LANDSCAPE RUG HOOKING

LANDSCAPE RUG HOOKING

A Painterly Approach to Creating the Landscapes You Love

DEANNE FITZPATRICK

Other Schiffer Craft Books on Related Subjects:

Jaana Mattson's Landscapes in Wool: The Art of Needle Felting, Jaana Mattson, ISBN 978-0-7643-6126-5

Organic Embroidery, Meredith Woolnough, ISBN 978-0-7643-5613-1

Create Naturally: Go Outside and Rediscover Nature with 15 Makers, Marcia Young, ISBN 978-0-7643-6434-1

Library of Congress Control Number: 2025930655

Designed by Christine B. Stuermer
Front cover design by Lindsay Hess
Photography by Angela Jorgensen and by Megan Lewis of Gallery 8 Photography
Type set in Quiet Sans / Fairplex Wide OT

ISBN: 978-0-7643-7001-4
ePub: 978-1-5073-0629-1
Printed in China

10 9 8 7 6 5 4 3 2 1

Published by Schiffer Craft
An imprint of Schiffer Publishing, Ltd.
4880 Lower Valley Road
Atglen, PA 19310
Phone: (610) 593-1777; Fax: (610) 593-2002
Email: Info@schifferbooks.com
Web: www.schifferbooks.com

ACKNOWLEDGMENTS

Angela Jorgensen manages Deanne Fitzpatrick Rug Hooking Studio. She has photographed and catalogued the rug images in this book and looked after so many details as we created this book. She is creative, intelligent, and talented and I love working in the studio with her.

Thank you to Jo Packham, who introduced me to Sandra Korinchak of Schiffer Craft. I told Jo I needed a publisher and she set up a meeting for me with Sandra. Sandra is a kind and supportive editor who really encouraged me and nurtured my vision for this book. Her notes were always welcome. She helped make this book so much better.

The designers Christine B. Stuermer, Lindsay Hess, and Kate North at Schiffer Craft made the book beautiful. And Megan Lewis, of Gallery 8 Photography, thanks for the pictures of me and for making me comfortable in front of the camera.

A thank you to the studio staff, our wonderful customers, and of course you the reader. I am so happy to be connected with all of you.

Putting this book together has helped me see the beautiful rustic quality of the land I live upon with my husband of 33 years, Robert Mansour. He is the keeper of our place, the planter, the trimmer, the mower. He has built the paths that are upon it and he is always in my heart.

▲ *Daisy Field and Goldenrod*, 12" × 12" (30.48 × 30.48 cm). The fields in this rug are hooked in small wavy lines with variegated yarn that lets there be many different greens. The daisies are hooked in a contrasting finer cream silk yarn that allows them to stand out. In the bottom, to establish a foreground, I used a contrasting color for the field. This use of the teal here allows me to show perspective, separating the foreground from the daisies through the use of color.

Landscape Rug Hooking

CONTENTS

▲ *Spruce in the Pasture*, 30" × 30" (76.2 × 76.2 cm). I can see the marsh beyond this pasture that is bordered by spruce trees and brush and scrub. The relatively straight horizon line shows that the land is flat, and the larger spruce before that land gives it perspective.

INTRODUCTION

Loving the Land You Live Upon

The land I live upon is part of a land grant from the 1700s that extends nearly 20 miles to the river near Oxford, Nova Scotia. Our little parcel of 7 acres is on a knoll in a dale, and the house upon it was built nearly two hundred years ago. In the spring it becomes a purple carpet of creeping Jenny, reminding me that many women lived here before me and nurtured this place. The old gray-shingled barn once held a red tractor, and it plowed for the root vegetable farm that was there before us. There is an apple orchard gone wild that blooms light-pink blossoms every June and litters the field with August whites at the end of summer. Hackmatacks, pine, spruce, cedar, and birch fill the tiny forests around our place. We built a pond about twenty years ago, and that brings some life to the place; foxes, ducks and geese, and deer are around.

This small bit of land is deceptive. Driving by it might look like a bunch of scrub and brush, but living on it season after season, year after year, it is indeed filled with inspiration. There is enough here to keep me making rugs for years. Yet, like any curious artist, I am inclined to go beyond it, to the sea, the mountains, the marshes, and the rivers that surround it.

Every time I drive in a car through the county that surrounds me, I am drawn to new ideas for landscape rugs. A single tree on a hill, cliffs with a little lighthouse perched upon them, a simple cottage lit by the sunset all call me to my frame. There is so much to see, so much to re-create in the form of hooked rugs.

And I want to make them all. I want to spend my life creating beauty. Taking the ordinary landscape and translating it into wool is a challenge that I have been taking upon myself for years. When my son was a boy of fourteen, he said, "Mom, your field rugs are your best rugs." He is over thirty now, and that comment has stuck with me more than the words of any curator or gallerist. You see, I believe that it is important to make work for those around us, and to make work about what is around us. I love that he saw the beauty in my landscape rugs. And I have come to agree with him. I love to show the natural world around me in my work. It is a way that I can make meaning out of my life.

We get the opportunity to reflect our days, our surroundings, our life back into our rugs. For me, that is essential. It is what it means to be an artist. We create, we re-create, we rerecord our lives through the simplest of means, with a hook and yarn and a piece of linen. We hook rugs.

And one of the most beautiful things we can hook is the landscape around us. I am compelled to do this. Sometimes when I walk down the road, I see the world in the texture of wool. I imagine just what wool I would use for the seedpod or the Queen Anne's lace. When we start hooking the landscape, we begin to see a world of color and texture. Cloth and yarn become a new way for us to paint the landscape: We paint it with wool.

In this book I will take you walking on a path through fields and dales, into the hills, through flower gardens and forests, and we will gaze at the sea and the sky as we wander through a painterly journey into hooking with yarn and wool cloth. You will learn how to translate the world around you into wool. Get ready for the adventure, because it is a big one. This is not just a how-to book about hooking landscape rugs, but it is also about how to see the landscape around you. I don't want to just show you how to hook an image that is exactly what you see out your window. In these chapters I want to help you see the potential that is in rug hooking and that is in you to capture your own vision, to capture in wool how you see the world.

NIGHT
SLOW FLUTE
WAYFARER
STAY?

▲ ***A Field with a Tinge of Red***, 30" × 30" (76.2 × 76.2 cm). It's the jumpy red outline of the leaves that makes them stand out so well. I love how that semicircular movement in the top right corner makes us feel the sky beyond what we see.

01

HOOKING THE LANDSCAPE

Landscapes are some of my favorite rugs to make because there is so much freedom in the hooking. Landscapes imply an expansiveness. I rarely hook a front yard; instead these field rugs are acres and acres of land. When I look at the landscape, I can easily take in 100 acres with my eyes and still see the details of it. In the following chapters you will learn how to find the balance between the expanse and the details in your own work.

I want to begin by telling you an overview of what I think is important in hooking these rugs. Throughout the book we will come back to and expand on these ideas.

When I hook landscapes, I begin by seeing and sketching. I often don't sketch exactly what I see. I have never really hooked rugs that were of a particular place. Instead they are reminiscent of a place. They are often a compilation of a beautiful tree from one place, a barn from another, and the gold field I saw on a drive two years ago. They feel like somewhere I have been, but they are not replica of it. I have photos for that.

My landscapes range in size from 3 by 5 inches to 5 by 6 feet and everywhere in between. The shapes are usually rectangles or squares. Years ago, I sometimes made rugs that were more sculptural, leaving the shape of the hills on the top as I omitted the sky. I have moved away from these simply because I so love to hook skies; I love how the sky gives more perspective. But you can explore that too, as I did. A landscape could be hooked in any shape: diamonds, circles, amoebas. It is up to you. The traditionalist in me loves the square and the rectangle, the traditional shape of hooked rugs since they were first made in the mid-1800s along the Eastern Seaboard of North America.

There is no definitive knowledge about where rug hooking started, but it is assumed that it began somewhere in New England, Quebec, or Atlantic Canada. It is seen as one of the few crafts that originated here in North America. I love that tradition, and as much as I like to push its boundaries, I respect it.

My rugs are made as art for the walls, but they can easily be made as rugs for the floor. I use wool material and yarn in my rugs and hook mostly on a linen backing. If I am hooking a rug for the floor, I like to use stronger coarse wools that will wear well. I avoid merino, fleece, and heavily textured yarn because, though they will last well in a floor rug, the loops flatten down and get an almost squashed look. I like the loops in my floor rugs to hold up. They will get a patina from being walked on, but you can still see the individual loops. You can use any wool in a floor rug; however, each wool will wear differently from being walked on, and this is important to consider. I bind my floor rugs differently than wall rugs, adding a piece of wool cloth on the back of them to protect them from wear. Sometimes I also add a traditional black cotton binding that is hand-sewn around the edges to

▲ *Little Village on the Edge of the Forest*, 8" × 29" (20.32 × 73.66 cm). The use of black outlines in the field adds depth. The light blue between the trees reshapes the trees and carries us into the sky.

protect the edges of the linen. These are important things to think about if you want to make floor mats.

When hooking landscapes, though, most of us are hooking it for the wall. The designs of landscapes are not so great for the floor. When they're placed on the floor, you can see the landscape from all sides, and you end up looking at it upside down or from the side. This is okay but not ideal. The very nature of landscape designs means they are best seen straight ahead. I think they belong on the wall.

I often refer to some of my landscapes as field rugs because that is what I see where I live. In rural Nova Scotia, I am surrounded by brush and scrub, wildflower and blueberry fields, and spruce trees. I know these things because I see them every day. Some of my landscapes are village rugs with layers of little houses and cottages, often near the sea. This is the other thing I know. I grew up in Newfoundland and still live near the sea. Sometimes these rugs show perspective, and sometimes I create them as a layered landscape, building one element on top of another with no interest in perspective or realism or even impressionism at all. In these rugs the creatures might be bigger than the houses. They are playful but they are also sometimes statements or stories.

Each rug I hook considers texture, color, design, and creativity. I don't sit and tick these off as boxes. It is not like that. As I draw, choose materials, and pull each loop through, there are decisions to be made. You are always making decisions when you hook rugs. Each time you change a color or move in a new direction, you have to make a decision. If you think too much, too long, or too hard about these, you will get bogged down. In landscape rugs I make decisions fast. After some time working on your landscapes, you will too, as you begin to rely on intuition and previous knowledge for this. For now, just focus on moving to the next loop. Make color and texture choices quickly and focus on getting the rug done. You will learn much more from the finished rug than you will from putting in a color and pulling it out too many times.

And here's why: Rug hooking is a forgiving craft. I love that about rug hooking. I love a craft that easily forgives you for your mistakes! Like life, we need to be able to experiment to learn. Our craft lets you make choices without holding you to any negative outcomes. I don't think I would enjoy a craft that did not let me experiment like this. Making mistakes is how art happens. That is why I encourage you to keep hooking rather than getting stuck on a particular color or area of your rug. Complete it. Once it is done, if the area still bothers you, you can go back and change it without it affecting the rest of the rug.

I hook in all different directions. I turn my frame so that I can get to different areas of the rug. I even hook upside down sometimes. I do not worry about precision and exactitude in these landscapes. They are organic and abundant like nature itself. I do not always hook in a particular direction for a particular element. There is no always. There is only mostly, and I feel free to change the direction of my hooking, the color, or the texture I am using at a whim. I do not hold myself to anything. I make marks on the rug with my hook as if they were brushstrokes. I work fast, sometimes with a bit of fury and sometimes with great intention. And I work. I always work. Almost everyday I show up at the frame, and this has been what has made the most difference in my work. More than anything else, showing up is what made me an artist.

▲ ***Centered Soul***, 30" × 25" (76.2 × 63.5 cm). Here the house exists as centered between two cliffs, a symbol of being in the middle of things, or of indecision. I see it as being between two places that I love. The house takes predominance over the landscape.

So I am not going to feed you recipes and give you hard-and-fast rules to make landscapes like mine, because I have never dealt in absolutes. I have reams of knowledge from years of making, and I am going to share that with you so that you can make landscapes that belong to you. Ones that reflect your world and your place in it. I will tell you how I hook, and ask you to watch to pay attention to how you hook.

To make great landscapes, you have to pay attention, not just to the suggestions in this book but to where you live, to what you know and love, and to your own reactions to what you see. As you hook, notice the directions you take, the type of lines and shapes you use, the shapes that you make as you hook, so you can make those marks your own. Pay attention to color around you and particularly how those colors make you feel. And it is not just colors that make your heart sing that you will need, but also those that make your soul plummet. The landscape around us brings up emotion and feeling, and you will use color in them to evoke this. You will use not only the colors you love, but the colors you need.

I remember once being on a Zodiac in the Bay of Fundy and feeling as if the cliffs along the coast were made of wool. When I look at the world, sometimes I see it in wool, and once you start hooking landscapes this will happen to you too. You will see goldenrod and think of the yarn in your stash that would be

perfect. We carry our rugs with us out into the world, and then we bring the world back to the frame. This is the promise of making. When we begin hooking landscape rugs, we will be forever changed and we will see the world differently. Beauty will be everywhere, and beauty will be enough. This is the promise of art. Sometimes we feel that our work must do more than be beautiful—that it must tell a story or make a statement—but I believe that beauty is something that can heal and soothe us, and it is something that we seek as humans. Beauty is important, and hooking landscapes allows us to focus on bringing beauty into the world.

Bushes, trees, little houses perched on cliffs, the colors of the beach rocks, the center of a flower: All will become great revelations. But it is not just the majestic that you will begin to take in more deeply; it is the ordinary. That was the great revelation to me—that I started to notice the colors of the gravel in the driveway, the grays and brown of the bark on a tree, the paint peeling off a piece of pipe on the ground. When I began hooking landscapes, my walks became discovery missions. Old dried-up seedpods became the first layer in my landscape. The form of last year's sunflowers standing in the garden began to look like queens of the land. The little foxes in the woods by the pond became iconic silhouettes. We all have so much to discover in our own little lives. Not one of us is ordinary. Each of us has miracles around us. Hooking landscapes helps us find them and see the majesty in our own lives.

◀ ***Deep into the Bay***, 42" × 25" (106.68 × 63.5 cm). This is how I see the cliffs of the Bay of Fundy near my home. In real life they are mostly brown, but up close and in my heart I see so many colors in these rugged rocks. Don't limit yourself to what you see in front of you. Be free with your imagination.

▲ ***Western Barns***, 10" × 16" (25.4 × 40.64 cm). Sometimes just hooking a few loops of a single color, such as the rose in this foreground field, is all it takes to imply flowers and create a focal point in the rug.

02

SEE THE LAND AROUND YOU

Basic Design Techniques for Hooking Landscape Rugs

It was on my walks over twenty years ago that I began to see the plain old farm fields along the Northumberland Strait for the beautiful landscapes that they really were. Bordered by wildflowers of lupin, tiger lily, and Queen Anne's lace, these fields I discovered were multilayered ecosystems that had so much life in them. Behind the wildflowers were cattails, brambles, and hayfields, and in the distance there might be an old orchard or a spruce forest. Each thing was beautiful on its own, but one leading into another really compounded the abundance and beauty of what I was seeing.

One day I went home and drew a 70-by-18-inch rectangle. In the upper corner I sketched in a simple Nova Scotia farmhouse, and then I began to scribble in a bit of grass, the essence of flowers in front of it, and big, sweeping lines for hills. And it began: my love affair with fields. This has been an enduring love. I have hooked hundreds of field rugs over the last two decades, inspired by that first field and every one I have seen after it.

When I walk, I watch. I take note. And this is critical to creating. You need to see, but you also need to observe the details and you need to record. Sometimes it is a quick series of snapshots on my phone. Other times, when I get home I draw what I remember and write little notes around it. My drawing skills are somewhat limited, so the notes help me remember what I saw.

We do not need to know how to draw to make great landscape rugs. It is more important that we remember and record so that we can re-create. Often I have not been able to draw something, but I can hook the wool to give you an impression of something. This is much more important. Do not let your feelings about how you draw to get in the way of making a great field rug. You can do it.

Designing rugs is not as much about drawing as it is about bringing elements together. Throughout this book I will show you that. You will learn how to design landscapes that do not rely on being an expert in drawing.

A good field rug is a story of the landscape, and we use wool, not words, to tell this story. So often I have not been able to draw something in nature, but when I draw with my hook it is a different story. The linen is on a bit of a grid. This helps me when I go to put a design on it. Sometimes it is much easier for me to get an idea when I hook than it is with a pencil on paper. So it is important to develop a trust in this process and go forth confidently, not worrying too much about whether or not you can draw a straight line. In fact, straight lines are rarely found in the landscape, so that should give you a head start. As important as it is to get some simple sketches on the linen to get you started, it is not the final drawing. It is just a guide. You can change it easily as you begin and continue your project.

Walk the Fields

I do two things nearly every day that are deeply connected to each other. I walk and I hook rugs. They may seem unrelated to each other, but they are not. They belong together. Through walking, I have come to see the landscape in a new way. Close-up and personal. I look into the woods as I walk down the road and see the moss underfoot, the fallen branches. I see the berry fields turning crimson. The sky meeting the spruce as well as the light falling through the birches all come back to my frame with me.

The walking, swinging my arms, moving my legs, feeling the wind on my face is important to my rug hooking. It keeps me in shape, and this is important. Rug hooking seems like a sedentary activity, but it takes a lot of physical energy, leaning in over the frame. You have to take care of your body, your hands, your neck, your shoulders. All will feel the strain if they are not nurtured. Walking eases the muscles and loosens my limbs and keeps me healthy to hook rugs. Find the movement that works best for you, whether it's outdoor stretches, chair yoga, or something else, and use it to supplement your rug hooking.

◀ *Three Spruce on Blueberry Barren*, 9" × 13.25" (22.86 × 33.65 cm). Contrasting colors and blending of the greens make this rug work. The tiny touches of mauve imply asters, and the gray implies rocks. You just need to get the idea across; not everything has to be outlined and distinguished.

This rug is a great example of how when you contrast materials, you can really make something stand out. The dull burnished gold in the narrow or worsted-weight yarn used in the middle ground and foreground is a striking contrast to the soft greens, not only in color but in sheen. Each wool has its own sheen, and this depends on the type of sheep it comes from as well as the way it is processed.

Why Designing Your Landscape Is Easy

Designing hooked rugs is easy. So easy, in fact, I was astounded the first time I discovered how. I could not believe that I could create my own designs right away. Before I was finished with my first little rug kit of four corner scrolls, I was already imagining what I could make on my own. Other crafts such as quilting and knitting require quite a complex level of skill before you can really think about designing your own creations. Weaving and cross-stitch require a lot of mathematical thinking. Most people would have to spend a good amount of time mastering the craft before they could even begin to think about designing their own personal work. In contrast, rug hooking allows you to begin creating your own designs as soon as you know how to pull a loop. It requires only a piece of backing, a black marker, and a little bit of magical thinking.

Planning Your Rug's Design

To design a hooked rug, you simply measure and mark off the area you want to hook on your backing. You normally draw a square or a rectangle, but other shapes are possible as well. It is very important that you leave some backing outside the square, so that your design can be attached to a frame. I always stretch my pattern on a hoop or a frame so it is tight like a drum and easy to hook on. You can use quilting hoops or attach the pattern to artist stretcher bars or an old wooden picture frame, using thumbtacks.

In recent years, my backing of preference has been linen, though I encourage beginners to use burlap. I used it myself for many, many years. It is economical and works well as a foundation. It is also the traditional foundation of rug hookers. Both my grandmothers hooked rugs in Newfoundland, an island province on the east coast of Canada. When rug hooking first began, women used the sacks that their potatoes or oats came in as backing, and the old discarded clothes from their household cut into strips. That is exactly what my grandmothers did. Burlap has a long and sturdy tradition in rug hooking. I now use linen because I sell my rugs, and I feel it is important to put them on the best backing I can. As a foundation, linen is stronger than burlap because it can tolerate getting wet. Water damage will rot burlap much more quickly. That said, I still like to hook on burlap. It feels traditional to me. For small decorative pieces and wall pieces, burlap is a fine backing, and it is easily accessible and much less expensive.

Linen or burlap often frays, so I zigzag-stitch or serge the edges of my backing to protect it from fraying. If you do not have a sewing machine or serger, you can just cover the edges by folding a piece of masking or duct tape over them. You can also leave the edges raw, but if you do, leave yourself 4 to 6 inches of extra backing material around the live area of your pattern. This protects the edge of the pattern from fraying. This is an important step because if you do not have border space around your pattern, it will be very difficult to stretch your pattern and hook your design to the edge. You will also need that extra backing area to bind your rugs when you have finished all the hooking. Binding is how you finish your rugs for the wall or the floor. I use a simple method of folding the fabric over twice to hide the serged or raw edges, then hand-sewing the edges as if I were hemming a pair of pants.

To create a design, simply draw or trace what you want to hook onto your backing. It is as easy as that. I take a Sharpie marker or a pencil and begin drawing some lines. Often I will go to my sketchbook and look through the drawings I have sketched out over the last few months, to decide what I want to hook, and then I will freehand it onto the linen. When I do this, the original drawing changes some. I do not try to get it perfect. This style of rug hooking is not made for perfection. It is made for process. The changes in the drawing are part of the process. I am not trying to re-create exactly what I drew in the sketchbook. Instead I am trying to re-create the inspiration that the drawing emerged from. You can take your own drawings and sketch them onto linen, and then you will be ready to start hooking your own landscape designs.

Sometimes people are intimidated with the idea of designing hooked rugs because they believe they cannot draw. Designing hooked landscape rugs often begins by drawing, but as I said earlier, you do not have to be good at it. So many of us have the idea that we cannot draw or we are not very creative. Early on in school, we began comparing ourselves to others, and if we did not see our talent quickly, we assumed it was not there. We saw the talent of others and decided that drawing was for them and not for us.

This exact thing happened to me as a child. My cousin Donny was a meticulous drawer, and he was praised for it by our teachers and the whole class. He spent hours with a pencil at home, as well as having a natural talent. By grade 2 I decided that drawing was his thing, and I stopped bothering with it. I liked to draw as a child, but because I did not draw as well as my cousin, I let it go.

This of course is the biggest barrier to beginning to design hooked rugs, and the one we have to overcome. Remember

Simple Understanding of Design Terms for Rug Hooking

Focal point is the area or item in the rug that is important and draws your eye. It can be in any part of the rug, and color is often used to emphasize it in hooked rugs.

Perspective simply means that the objects closer to you appear larger and the ones further away appear smaller. It helps us understand scale and can make a landscape look more realistic.

Balance means that your rug does not appear to heavily weighted in one area. The elements of the design are positioned throughout the design in a way that considers their weight and keeps our eyes travelling around the rug. Both color and texture are used to create balance in hooked rugs.

Movement means that there is action in your rugs. You hook in marks and lines that create motion and feeling in your work.

Pattern and *repetition* mean that we use similar or the same shapes over and over again throughout the rug. A shape repeated throughout the landscape, such as the curve of a hill, can create this. Your landscape rugs may not contain pattern or repetition often, but you can use these techniques to create imaginative landscapes that are less realistic and more playful, traditional patterns to make landscapes more imaginative and story based.

▲ *Sunlit Spruce*, 33.25" × 17" (84.455 × 43.18 cm). The sky is a place to decorate and play with. I imagined daisies as clouds. As well, In this row of seven trees, there is the symbolism of being one of seven sisters.

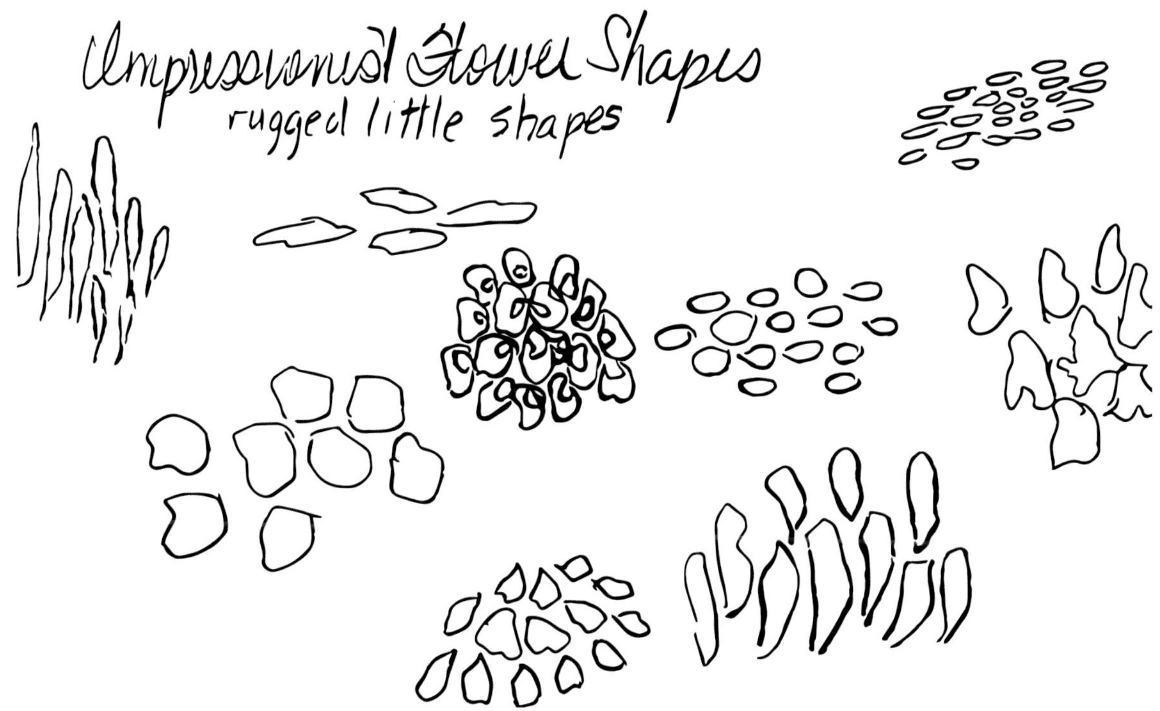

drawing is just a technical skill that gets better with practice. It was not until I became a rug hooker that I began to draw again. I started where I left off, but over time with practice and after filling many sketchbooks I began to see that I drew a certain way and had a certain style that really was perfect for rug hooking. I like to make contour drawings that show the outline of the subject rather than the details, and this is what rug hooking requires. We create the details as we hook.

To design hooked rugs you do not have to be a talented artist. You just need to know how to hold a pencil and make a mark, and you have to be willing to take a chance. It is something we can start simply with. And by starting simple we reassure ourselves that we are indeed full of possibilities. With each design we go a little further along.

You can start with a pen on a paper napkin. All that matters is that you start. In fact my first sketch book was a lined Hilroy notebook like the ones I used in elementary school to write my alphabet. Don't get caught up in supplies, just put a pencil or pen to paper. If you have not practiced drawing for a long time you might, like me, begin where you left off. You might draw a tree the same way you drew one when you were eight. That's okay. It is a great place to start and it might be just where you need to be. Rug hooking requires simple drawings, ones that can be hooked with wool, loop after loop. The simpler the lines the more you can rely on the many different textures of wool to enhance the rug, In fact, a heavy pencil sketch that is perfectly rendered with hundreds of lines would be difficult to hook. You want to keep it simple.

Rug hooking itself is a craft you can master because you only need to learn one stitch. You can begin designing within minutes of learning. A simple tree drawn upon a square can get you started designing landscape rugs. One line drawn across your rectangle can divide it into land and sky. From there it is your imagination and your color work that will carry it away.

The basic principles of design such as focal point, perspective, balance, movement, pattern and repetition (see text box, page 14) can be learned and used in creating your designs. I use these principles every day and they will come up in this book from time to time. But don't be daunted by them. You can just consider them. Just remember there is a strong tradition in rug hooking of throwing away these principles and hooking what you like.

I love this wild freedom in rug hooking. In antique mats you will often see a cat as big as a house or a large bird sitting on the roof. Women drew their designs freely without particular attention to the traditional rules of design and made beautiful rugs. We often see a lack of inhibition in these early rugs that is enviable. Traditional rugs, because they have often been designed for the floor, are a flat lay design with elements arranged flatly across the area without attention to perspective. Try not to get weighed down with loads of information about design techniques. I never learned these until years after I began creating my own designs. Right now with the internet, information is at our fingertips and we can learn a lot quickly. I have found that sometimes this hinders early learners rather than helps them. The best way to learn about designing and hooking rugs is by making them.

When creating landscape designs I often have a focal point or a lead in to the rug. Sometimes it is a tree or a house in the lower left hand corner. In my early rugs I did not even know that this was a focal point, or the point in your rug that draws the eye; I just naturally drew it. I do think of perspective, which simply means that things that are closer appear larger. I will often use color to show perspective as well, making things in the background darker, and land in the foreground lighter.

I use what I know about design but they are not my only tools. Like the early settlers who hooked mats to warm cold

Hook Yourself a Sampler

It is very important to get to know what a particular wool can do.

You can create a personal stash sampler for yourself that will help you know and understand the wools you have.

1. **Draw a 10-by-10-inch square on your backing.**
2. **Divide it with ten lines one inch apart, horizontally and vertically, creating 100 smaller squares.**
3. **Outline all the squares in a dark color such as black, navy or eggplant.**
4. **Hook one square with each yarn in your stash so you can see what It looks like. It might sound like a lot to have 100 types of yarn or cloth in your stash, but you will find that it accumulates quickly. If you only have ten now, start the sampler and hook a new square every time you add a yarn to your stash.**

You can staple a piece of each yarn you use and its number and name to a piece of card stock as a key to show you what the yarn looked like before it was hooked. You can number the yarns left to right to coordinate with the squares that you hooked. Some people will need a color key to remember the wool before and after, while some will naturally remember. Do what works for you.

If your stash is already large, you can also start a second sampler so you can add hooked samples of any new yarns you add to your stash.

Once you have filled all the squares, you can bind and finish your sampler and use it as a table mat or chair pad in your home, or you can sew it face to face to a piece of wool and stuff it with filling to create a little pillow for your hooking chair.

You don't have to limit yourself with this exercise. If squares don't interest you, you could create a similar sampler but draw 100 tiny houses, or trees, or circles, and then hook a background around them. Imagine the rugs or pillows you could make. I once created a larger rug like this by dividing the foreground into a patch work of farmers fields and hooking each one in a different material. The important thing is to make it a sampler: that is, each wool is used just once.

This sampler will be a reminder of what the yarns you have can do in your landscape rugs and you will see them clearly. Knowing your stash helps you use it well and gives our imagination a boost when we are hooking. We know what we have and what we can choose to use it well for the landscapes we are making.

floors I do not rely heavily on these things. In my landscapes sometimes the house is perched between two cliffs and the trees are as big as the house. I let my mind be free and I create dreamscapes as well as landscapes. When we hook landscapes there is room for interpretation. As an artist you can show the landscape the way you see it in your mind. In fact, getting at the way you see it is sometimes much more interesting than the way it actually is.

Most of my landscapes are not of a particular place but a composite of places I have been or seen over my life. I like to sketch my ideas from my head rather than from a picture, since this gives me room to add my stories and my ideas. The hooked landscapes become less about realism. In fact, I would say that over time I have become less and less interested in depicting how things actually are in the landscape and more and more interested in showing how I see the world in my rugs.

Traditionally landscape art has been about reflecting back to the viewer what they are already seeing. There is so much good work in this tradition. However I am more captivated by landscape art that makes us feel the place, that pours over the details and the minutia of a place and then makes us feel what

◀ *Farmers Fields*, 27" × 25" (68.58 × 63.5 cm). This is a sampler rug. I outlined each field in a dark color and then played with my yarns to see what each yarn could do. It is a great way to learn the possibilities of your stash of yarn.

▲ *The Field Moon*, 37.5" × 13.5" (95.25 × 34.29 cm). This rug has everything I love. The sketchy outlines around the moon make it a stronger focal point and lets it compete with the barns for a place in the rug. Notice the use of multicolored textured yarns in the field and how it draws us into the rug.

it is like to be in that place. I feel this is true in the work of Canadian artists Emily Carr and The Group of Seven. They are more about feeling than thinking. I have been influenced by this and have tried to bring it into my art.

This approach to hooking landscape rugs has developed over a long time. I have been hooking rugs for thirty four years and some of my very early rugs were primitive landscapes. I hooked a few houses on a hillside over looking the bay, remembering my childhood home. Even in those very early rugs I knew it was impossible to depict them exactly. For that I could take a photograph.

Bringing the Wool into the Picture

I learned early that wool has its limitations. It is like working with a chunky marker or a broken crayon rather than a fine point marker. Knowing your medium, appreciating and respecting it for what it is will take you a long way in your art. That does not mean that you should not push it and try hard, you definitely should. It is clear though that you should figure out what a particular wool can do, and then do that with it. Within the medium of rug hooking we are working with many different textures and weights of wool, and each one is good for many things. As I choose wools for the landscape I am not only looking at their color, which of course is of primary importance, I am also looking at how that wool will hook and how that could fit into the landscape. Each wool can offer something different and it is important to be able to see in your mind's eye what they all look like hooked.

The Sketchbook

The most important design tool you will ever have is your sketchbook. Start one right away if you want to hook landscapes. Don't wait until you believe you can draw to start. Most people feel they cannot draw well. Start now. As soon as you get interested in rug hooking is the time to start collecting your sketches. If you wait until you can draw, you will never get there.

I have stacks of sketchbooks, filled, though not always to the brim. Sometimes I leave an old book with three or four pages left in them for the joy of beginning again. Everyone loves to start a new book. Sometimes when I go back to them, because going back to review them is very important, I finish them up, not wanting to waste the paper. Your sketchbooks are a record of your creative life. They can hold our thoughts and ideas, and they store the wealth of our imagination.

I draw whenever I feel like it. Drawing helps me focus. If I am listening to someone speak, having a pencil in my hand really lets me listen well. If I am waiting for someone in the car, I can pull a sketchbook out of my knapsack. In a restaurant there is always the dinner napkin. Every scrap of paper that you mark on has the chance to be a hooked rug. Sometimes when I watch TV at night, I pull out my sketchbook and do quick, loose contour drawings of things I see on the screen. I try to integrate it into my life by leaving pencils and sketchbooks around and available. They are on my desk, in my bag, in the car. When I need one, I can find one quickly and easily.

I want to sketch daily, but I don't and I might never. I just like to know that there is a sketchbook close at hand and I can grab it whenever I feel moved to draw. Do what feels right for you, making sure that the sketchbook is part of your creative practice, those things that you do on a regular basis that make you better at your art and your craft. It is essential to designing your landscapes. I have a sketchbook with a pencil on my desk all the time, and one in my backpack that I carry with me.

In the last few years, I have been keeping my work and daily notes in unlined books so I can also draw in them. Writing and

Five Rough Sketches

Draw each of these in one minute or less. Set a timer on your phone and draw each one for a minute. When the time is up, turn the page and start with the next one. Don't judge yourself or try to be accurate. Just use your memory and your pencil. Ready. Set. Go.

1. Your backyard
2. The view out your window from childhood
3. The trees along a highway
4. The last time you were near the water, a pool, a lake, a river, the sea
5. A view in your neighborhood

I hope you surprised yourself with this exercise. It is a great way to loosen up our imaginations and get the pencil flowing.

Three Exercises for an Inspired Sketchbook

I love that my sketchbooks show me that this is my style, and show me how I see the world. Once we start a habit of looking and of sketching how we see the world and reimagine it in our drawings, it will lead to an endless amount of rug possibilities. Landscape rug hooking is full of design possibilities, and so are you.

I encourage people to begin designing their own landscape rugs. Think of the landscapes you have seen, the ones you grew up with, the ones you know intimately now. How can you reimagine these into hooked rugs? There is a great freedom in hooking your own designs, and you can begin with these simple ideas.

- **Take old photographs from trips and draw from them.**
- **Take an art book and look at the composition of a painting. Reimagine that composition in a place that you know.**
- **Take an image from your photos or an art book and add something to it, such as a person, a tree, houses.**

sketching belong together. Our notes annotate our drawings and tell us what was on our mind, what was happening around us. You can write down times, dates, and places beside the drawing. Make notes about the colors. You will find that these little annotations bring the drawings to life, triggering your memory, and help you recall and see more clearly.

Here is the thing I have learned about sketching. The first two or three or sometimes six or seven are rarely ever any good. Your hand and your mind need time to warm up. Don't be afraid if the first six or seven quick sketches of landscapes do not resonate with you. You will often feel at first that you have drawn this a hundred times before. Especially when you are drawing from your head. When you begin drawing again, you will rely on all the shapes and compositions you have used before and favor. When you keep at it, these begin to morph into new ideas. It takes practice, and practice takes time. Your practice will lead you to good designs.

If you do not know what to draw, use prompts such as photographs or art and photography books. Rough sketches are great. Just keep on doing it for a while, and you will find that as your hands warm up, your sketches get better and so does your imagination. One sketching session with thirty drawings will often leave me with only two or three design possibilities. And it is very rare that those are in the first four or five sketches. Warming up is part of the process.

I do not draw well or accurately, but I do draw. This is what is important. If you are just starting, you must suspend your judgment about what you draw, and you have to accept that practice is what you are missing. Once you keep drawing, you will get better. And remember what I said earlier in this book: You do not have to be a good drawer to design good rugs. If I depended on my drawing skills as an artist, I would have given up long ago. Drawing leads me into my rugs, and it helps develop my skills. It helps me see what I know, and this is good practice for hooking rugs.

Once you have been drawing for a while, reviewing your old sketchbooks is also important. There is really no point in keeping things if we do not go back to them once in a while. Over time, I have gone back to sketchbooks and found some jewels that I drew years before. We are not always ready to hook our drawings. Sometimes that comes a little later. Our sketchbooks capture our design history. They tell us what we were interested in, how we saw something, and they are essential to designing rugs that capture the work we know.

Showing Up

Getting things done takes discipline. And it isn't easy. I have to discipline myself to get things done in the yard, and to clean the house. And as much as I like to write, as good as it often feels, it takes a lot of discipline from me.

Showing up is the key to doing anything well. You can show up and write (well or poorly) or draw (well or poorly). You can show up and just give the living room a lick and a prayer. It may not be daily, but if you show up consistently, it amounts to something.

I have learned this from my hooking. I have made a few thousand rugs, I would guess. I have no idea, really. Never counted. Each rug I make was dependent on the rugs that came before it. Some of the rugs along the way were beautiful, and some were just fine. If I had kept a record and could see an image of each rug in the order that I made them, I would see a progression, because each rug grows a little from the last one I made.

I show up even when I don't feel like it. Because showing up is not about the breath of inspiration calling you to the frame. Showing up is about commitment and love. It is also about work. I don't wait for the muse to take me by the hand.

"Inspiration exists, but it has to find you working," said Pablo Picasso. And I believe it is true. It is in working itself that ideas come. It is because I am here with the pen or the hook in hand that the muse whispers in my ear. It is because I am on my fifth or tenth bad sketch that a good sketch emerges. These are all collected together in my sketchbook, and when I need an idea, I can go to it.

I am not able to go search for an idea out of thin air because I want and one. It does not work for me like that. Ideas stew. They build on thoughts, experiences, things we hear, smell, and see, and these all blend together. Sometimes in a rug you will have no idea where the idea is coming from until you are done. And then you can see it fully, and it will remind you of something in your life.

Sometimes you cannot see it at all, and then one day you will see something or feel something in your life that reminds you of your rug.

This is when you know you are working. And that your consistent ability to show up is helping yout art grow. This is true for most disciplines.

A lot of things are built on showing up. Friendships grow because we show up for each other, talents and skills improve, houses get cleaner, jam gets made, love gets stronger.

"I show up even when I don't feel like it."

▲ ***Water Shimmers***, 8″ × 18″ (20.32 × 45.72 cm). This is a single-color landscape hooked only in shades of blue turquoise. Even the outline is a darker shade of blue instead of a traditional black. I also used a bit of shimmer in a synthetic yarn as a detail.

03

DRAWING THE SIMPLEST LANDSCAPE

The best way to start hooking the landscape is to keep it easy and simple. Instead of trying to re-create your favorite place, you might begin by loosening up your rug-hooking muscles. I have a simple technique that I use to create landscapes. It is especially effective for people who are just beginning to hook landscape rugs. Instead of worrying about making your piece look like someplace you know, you can focus on learning how to create a bit of movement and depth in a simple four-part landscape.

STEP 1:

Draw a 5-by-7-inch rectangle on your linen. Hold your pencil at the top, so you do not have a strong grip on it, and you will get a nice, loose line. I love soft, slightly curvy lines. They suit the landscape and let you show movement in your rugs.

Leaving the top quarter of the rectangle empty for the sky, simply draw three slightly wavy lines across the rest of the rectangle. They do not have to create equal-sized areas. You can choose.

In the bottom area, write "foreground." Moving up, in the second area, write "middle ground," and in the third area, write "background." In the top quarter, write "sky."

If you want, you can draw a circle or quarter moon in the sky, but it is not necessary.

STEP 2:

Now choose light, medium, and dark shades of a single color. I like to use mixed shades for each of these areas, but you could try it with a single shade, or even just two shades. It could be greens or blues, yellows or reds. I have played with all kinds of colors.

STEP 3:

Put the lightest shade in the foreground, the next lightest in the middle ground, and the darkest shade in the third area. Going from light to dark will really help create depth and perspective in your little rug.

When you hook these shades in, hook them horizontally rather than vertically. You want to follow the lines you have created, using the line you drew as a guide. Here is the trick though: You do not want to follow them exactly, so that your rug hooking is too linear. I like to hook and follow the curve of the line along about three-quarters of the line and turn back, then hook it halfway back and stop. This keeps my hooking from becoming too predictable. It also lets me use the lines as a guide rather than a definitive recipe.

Then put in another piece of wool in the same or similar shade and start again, mimicking your original hand-drawn line.

STEP 4:

Keep adding new wools in a linear way, following this idea but creating new starting and finishing points all the time.

Be careful not to hook in clumps or up and down as you begin to fill the area. Keep your movement flowing across the piece.

Avoid hooking in straight lines across the rug.

Once the areas are nearly full, you might have to fill in small spots in an upward motion, but that will be okay because you have established your movement and horizontal by that time.

Step 5:

In the top quarter you can hook in shades of blues for a sky. I often choose a pale blue.

I like to hook the sky in small cloudlike areas that are a bit fuller than the more curvy linear hooking in the fields and hills. This changes how the sky looks compared to the field, and gives it a different kind of textural quality and movement. It makes it look more like sky and less like the rest of the land.

You can use cream or yellow, or a million other shades, to hook in a moon, a sun, or a few stars.

Have a bit of fun with these. I like making them in a single color, but you could do it in fall, spring, or summer shades too, using different colors in each of the three sections. There is no perfect way, and there are many good ways.

Experiment with the distance between your lines, the movement in your lines, and the colors you use. This simple design could lead to many unique rugs.

▲ *Golden Rod Beach*, 11" × 5" (27.94 × 12.7 cm). A rug does not have to be big to have impact. Four strong colors—fern green, gold, royal blue, and sky blue—hooked in layers gives us a definitive sense of beauty and place in this little rug.

The Three Grounds

A good way to think about hooking landscapes is to think of your image as foreground, middle ground, and background. This will help you show perspective through the use of color. In a simple beginner landscape, the foreground is often the lightest color, and it has a little room to add elements such as bushes, flowers, or even a house. It is the part of the design that is closest to you. The middle ground is between the foreground and the background and uses midlevel colors. Any objects placed here will appear smaller than those in the foreground. It is often seen as the field, or the acreage behind the house, for example. The background is the part of the landscape that meets the sky, and it is farthest away. For this you can use the darkest colors. It is often seen to be back hills, trees, or mountains.

▲ ***Well-Loved Fields***, 13" × 9" (33.02 × 22.86 cm). This rug is also made up of three simple lines, but they do not go straight across the rug. You can also see here that I have used curlicues in the sky to imply an impending storm.

In the sky, I drew a few lines that were swirled to give me some direction. I then hooked along these lines various shades of light blue. I gathered up all my blues for this sky, and a little white, using a variety of strands and textures and even a little sparkle. You'll notice that I used the sparkly merino yarn to accent the swirls. There are only slight color differences, but because the emphasis was on hooking in the swirly lines, this sky works. It is also about the direction in which I hooked.

◀ ***Seascape***, 8" × 8" (20.32 × 20.32 cm). The big, thick, soft pale-green merino yarn in this tiny landscape feels like flowers or grass that you want to explore, and the curved black line draws you beyond the foreground in this small rug.

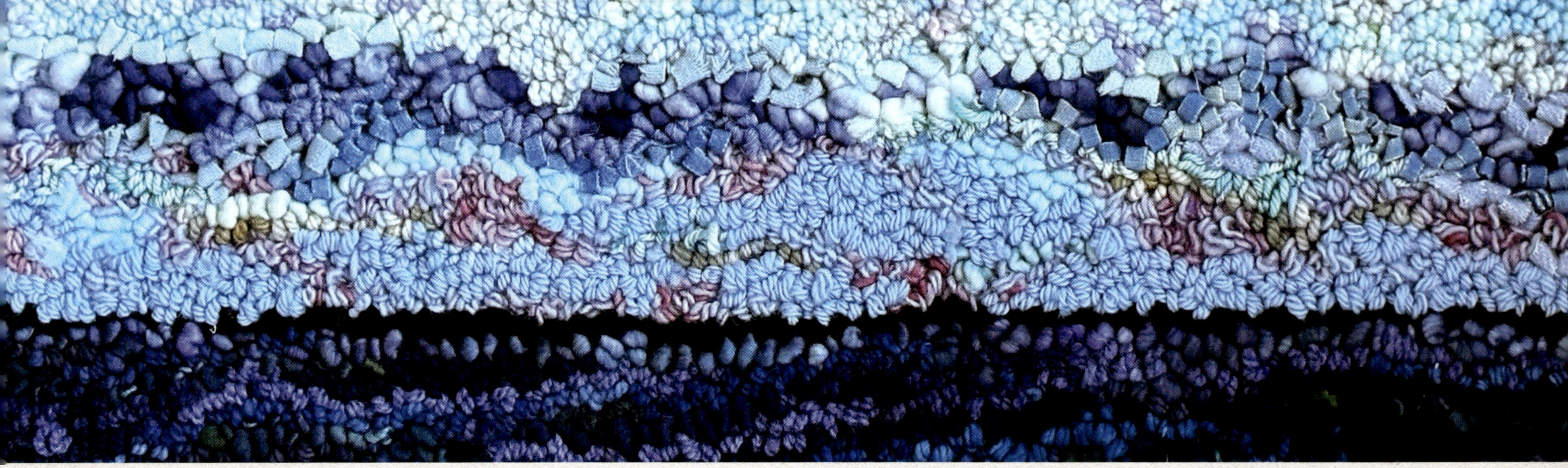

▲ ***Sea and Sky Forever***, 21" × 7" (45.72 × 22.86 cm). This is such a simple design. The work is done by hooking directionally in a way that reflects the sea and the sky. The bits of pink in the sky really capture your attention and make you wonder: Is it sunrise or sunset?

For the sky, I first hooked in a very thick blue yarn with some pink fit in, and I hooked thick lines of this all the way across, in random 3-inch-long lines. I used four strands of this wool, so it was puffy. I then gathered a selection of light blues and moved them in and around the puffy yarn. As I headed toward the middle of the sky, I brought in some medium blues and some hand-cut cloth to add some drama before going back to the lighter blues again. This worked beautifully to take a very simple idea and turn it into an interesting landscape.

Horizon Skyline Landscapes

You can create a landscape with a single line drawn straight across a rectangle. This creates a horizon line for a flat landscape such as prairie, and it also works well for the sea. This is the simplest landscape to draw. I like to position the line about one-quarter or one-third from the bottom of your rectangle. You can also position the line at two-thirds of your rectangle. Depending on where the line is, there will be more or less sky. I do caution you not to create a line straight across the middle of your rectangle, since this can be difficult in terms of design. It is harder to get the idea of landscape across if the line is in the middle, because our eye is drawn to the center and not to the whole rug.

For the sea or the land, I choose two to six shades of related colors. In the sea, I used six blues and hooked slightly wavy lines across. For the canola fields, I used only three colors, but they were all hand-dyed golds, and I hooked this area across but angled my lines of yarn toward the black horizon line, which is always hooked first in these landscapes.

These are two-part landscapes, field or sea and sky. And it is in the sky where we are given freedom to be playful and create interest. The sky makes up approximately two-thirds to three-quarters of these landscapes, so you have the chance to use it to create impact.

I think these rugs are beautiful in their simplicity. I have only ever hooked them small, but I think they could be done larger, using more wools and emphasizing more interest in the sky design. They create a sky area that leaves us the opportunity to decorate or play in, rather than creating traditional clouds and blue sky, though this could work too. I am always looking for opportunities to let my hook roam freely across a space, and this idea is perfect for this. You can let these landscapes be very simple, or you can make them very interesting and complex. The simple flat horizon line creates perspective, and we then use color to enhance that if we want. However, when a rug has only one single line in it, that line is strong and it does a lot of work on its own to create perspective.

◀ *Canola on the Island*, 18" × 9" (45.72 × 22.86 cm). Driving down the road, I was struck by a farmer's yellow canola fields, and I wanted this rug to be only about that field under a blue sky. There was nothing else I wanted to show, and a single line across the horizon worked perfectly for this design.

Blue Hills Landscape: Creating a Landscape with a Few Simple Lines

You can create strong, majestic landscapes with a few simple lines. These rugs can be any size. The key is to show the soft hills and valleys with your loosely drawn lines. The completed rug looks more complicated than the original drawing because, really, all the work for this piece is done in the hooking. I have chosen blues for this rug, but you could choose your favorite color.

1. You can draw your design with a pencil at first so you can easily redraw it later.
2. Choose the areas you want to outline.
3. You can outline with interesting yarns, not just black.
4. After you choose what to outline in your landscape, begin hooking in the fields.
5. You can see close-up how to layer and blend your yarns.
6. You will need a variety of textures and colors to create your landscape.
7. If you want to retrace your pencil drawing, you can use a Sharpie marker.
8. Your colors are hooked close together and blended with each other, so that it is hard to tell where one color starts and another ends.
9. Completed rug: a blue landscape.

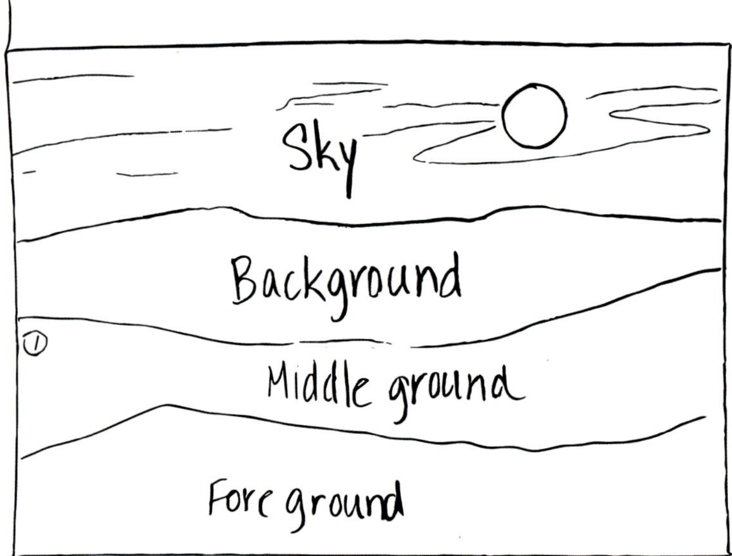

STEP 1: MAKE A LIGHT DRAWING

Drawing the design on with pencil softens it and makes it less intimidating. Hold the pencil firmly, with your hand near the top—you have a little less control and your line will be gentler, while the firmness of your grip will ensure you make a good mark.

Draw three or more lines across your pattern area, holding your pencil loosely so that the lines have a little movement in them. Think of the shapes of hill, fields, and trees as you add extra lines. Keep it simple though. You do not have to draw these in. You want to create a rolling landscape, and your simple flowing lines will do this.

I like the impermanence of the pencil. I don't always use it, but especially when I am unsure of my design, I want room to change it. The pencil is less final and gives you room to interpret the design.

STEP 2: CHOOSE WHAT TO OUTLINE

Don't agonize over the choice. When you're going to pick a color, there is no "one color." Just start off by picking one to three colors and begin outlining.

Sometimes just for outlining, I pick an amazingly interesting yarn or fabric because it adds something special to the rug. For this one I have picked a merino worsted weight, and a merino chunky that is wrapped with a thread, both of which are hand-dyed. I'll go back and forth between the two throughout the outlining.

I don't outline every pencil mark, and sometimes I don't go right to the edge. I freely interchange the two outlining yarns that I chose, without a lot of planning or thought. When I use a thin yarn such as the worsted weights, I'll often use two strands.

Go ahead and hook your outline like an adventure; the outline, in a landscape of hills and dales, lets you cordon off acres of land by creating boundary lines. That is essentially what the outline is: a chance to distinguish one area of the landscape from another.

Hook a solid line but leave a little space in between the loops, so you can have a little movement in those lines. Sometimes I overlap the lines, intertwining them a bit because it makes my landscape lines sketchy, and I like this. After the basic outline, fill in some extra little sketchy lines that you think look good—it will add some depth.

STEP 3: LOVE THE FIRST COLOR

After you finish the outline, choose a yarn that you love, one that interests you. I am often affected by the outline color for my first choice. This first color choice sets the color tone for the rug, so know that and let it inform your choice, but don't let fear get in the way or slow you down. Take a chance.

You can use this color in a single area, or sometimes, if I love it, I use it across the width of the whole mat. I might use it all across, but I might not use only one yarn for a whole area (or acreage) that is outlined. I will often use two or more yarns within one outlined area.

I like to leave this first color out and ready to use again in the other areas of the landscape. I might come back to it.

STEP 4: BRING ON THE COLOR

You have established something. You made your first sketch and then sketched it again with your beautiful outline. Yay!

Now I like to bring in the color. I will go to my stash and add a few colors in. Though I have set a tone with the color of my outline and my first choice, there are still many directions to go in.

The American rug-hooking teacher Nola Heidbreder says that she likes to audition colors for her rugs. I love this idea. I go to my stash and lay colors down on the mat to see which ones sing to me. You can use technical tools such as the color wheel, but the audition is the best way to do this.

Go to your stash and lay two colors on a piece of linen. Now add one other color, take it away, add another. Keep doing this and pay attention to each audition, thinking how each color change affects the other two colors. It is great practice for choosing colors.

I take a "know it when I see it" approach. However, "knowing it" has come with years of practice.

As I was choosing colors for this rug, the evening light came by my window. I decided that it was time to set it aside for the morning. The daylight, the natural light, really allows me to choose colors better. So often I have persisted at dusk and introduced a new color only to have to surrender it in the morning when it looks so different.

Instead of hooking in new colors in the evening, when I cannot see as well, I just lay a few colors on the frame before I leave for the evening. They are there, ready to audition in the morning. I come back "mise en place," with everything ready to go, when I return to the frame. This habit keeps me happy and lets me take the next step, without wasting time picking and hooking the wrong color.

STEP 5: DON'T NEED TO BE SURE

Keep adding new colors all around the rug—one color at a time. In this rug, I went deeper to teals, since it was a natural step from the blues.

This is the "I don't know what I'm doing" phase. It will feel like you are unsure and a bit lost. You will put in a wool and take it out; you will make mistakes and find that some choices will be taken out altogether. I do this all the time. Learn to become comfortable in being lost.

It is interesting that the foreground or focal point comes later when I hook a rug like this. For this rug the focal point will be in the front left corner to the middle of the rug. I like to reserve this area until I get the color established in the rug as a whole. This is not the only way to approach focal point. It is one way of doing it that I tend to use. Once I have added six to ten shades all over the rug, I will often put in a bush, flowers, branches, etc. as an area of interest. In this piece I used a Sharpie marker to draw in some seedpods or plants. I used the Sharpie to make it a clear and permanent drawing. I could easily still change it as I hooked; however, I wanted clear direction.

▲ ***Blue Chrysanthemum Landscape***, 18" × 9" (45.72 × 22.86 cm). Here you can see the whole rug I was working on in the previous pages' steps. I began with one color and chose a few more to go with it each step of the way. It is important to commit to a palette as we create landscape rugs because it gives us guidance on what to choose next.

▲ ***Neutral Landscape***, 30" × 10" (76.2 × 25.4 cm). This is a simple three-line landscape that is layered using only neutral tones. When all the colors are tonally the same, it is important to distinguish them with the depths and the intensity of the shades and with texture.

We Belong to the Land

The year that I turned forty, I returned home to the little town that I grew up in in Newfoundland with a childhood friend. We went back to our hometown for three days just to visit. Together we walked through graveyards, on the beaches, and down the roads we had so often traveled. We each took time to ourselves to go back to our own spots.

I grew up on Old Settlement hill in a three-story clapboard house that felt as if it was tilting toward the sea. Behind it was a hill of rock and shoddy-looking spruce. The view out the front window, though, was perfect. It gazed down over a little valley of houses and a beach, a bay, a distant village, and dark-green hills. I can close my eyes today and see it all just as it was. I spent so much time in those front windows watching the comings of goings of that place that I have it committed to memory. It is my beautiful place.

On my second day home, I decided to take the half-hour walk all the way to the top of the hill. I just wanted to see every little house, all the rocks and fields I had left behind. As I walked the hill, I took it all in. I remembered who lived where, and I took in the views from every spot.

It was not a place of fancy things or fancy people. It was just as it was, you know, homemade bread and raisin buns, tea, and too much whiskey. There were little sheds in people's yards where the men seemed to carry out their days; in fact, it seemed as if the men lived in those sheds. The women went to bingo, and to church, and to the little shops to get a bit of meat for supper. Fish was gotten off the boats when they came in to shore. It was a beautiful place with a culture all its own, but there was never much fancy about it.

After I got to the top of the hill, I took a little breather and headed back down. About a third of the way down, just as I came out if the woods and before I got to Pius Murphy's general store and could see the sea again, I began to hear opera music coming out the windows of a little house on the right. I felt as if I might be in a dream. It was beautiful. It was also a realization. It was in that moment that I realized that places change. The land may remain the same, but the people in it change.

When I was growing up there, we had never heard of opera music. The music pouring out of a little house set back in a field would have been traditional fiddle or accordion music. I suddenly saw that though the land might feel the same to me, and I might feel that I belong to it, the land no longer belongs to me. I also began to feel that my affection for the land was in me, and the land belonged only to itself. It is not waiting for our return, though the sound of opera music that day did feel like a special climax in a film about returning. The land never misses us, but we miss it.

And I take that with me as I imagine and create the landscapes in my hooked rugs. They are places that are meaningful to me, and the way I feel them, the way I see them, is more important to convey than the way they actually are.

> "The land never misses us, but we miss it."

▲ *Rocky Beach Tree*, 11" × 15" (27.94 × 38.1 cm). If you are having trouble distinguishing one element of your rug from another, try using a contrasting bright outline such as the yellow that outlines the branches here.

04

FOLLOW THE LINE

The Importance of the Outline

Over the years, I have hooked hundreds of landscape rugs. Each one its own little place with its own little story. One of the challenges in making them is always about how to outline the rug.

Outlining has a long, hard-and-fast tradition in rug hooking. For years in traditional hooked mats, everything was outlined. In fact, the "rules" were that you would outline each object in the mat in one color, most often black, and fill it in using another color.

This might be familiar to those of us who colored as children. I remember using my green crayon and pressing hard to outline the edge of a leaf, then filling it with the same crayon but using it softly. In rug hooking, outlining was used to distinguish each object in the mat and separate it from the background.

The history of rug hooking has a lot to teach us as we make landscape rugs. The simplicity of this technique still matters a lot in making rugs today. However, when we are hooking landscape rugs we need to use a lot of discretion with outlining. Landscape rugs can sometimes require a more painterly style than traditional hooked rugs, and we can almost forget about outlining altogether, but not quite. I find that I still sometimes need a bit of outlining even in the most painterly rugs.

Outlining is the line of your rug, and our lines are often the foundation of our design. We often underestimate the value of outlining, thinking of it as an old-fashioned, traditional way of hooking, but in rug hooking it is foundational. I consider it as the bones of my rug and a way to give the rug structure. What could be more important than that?

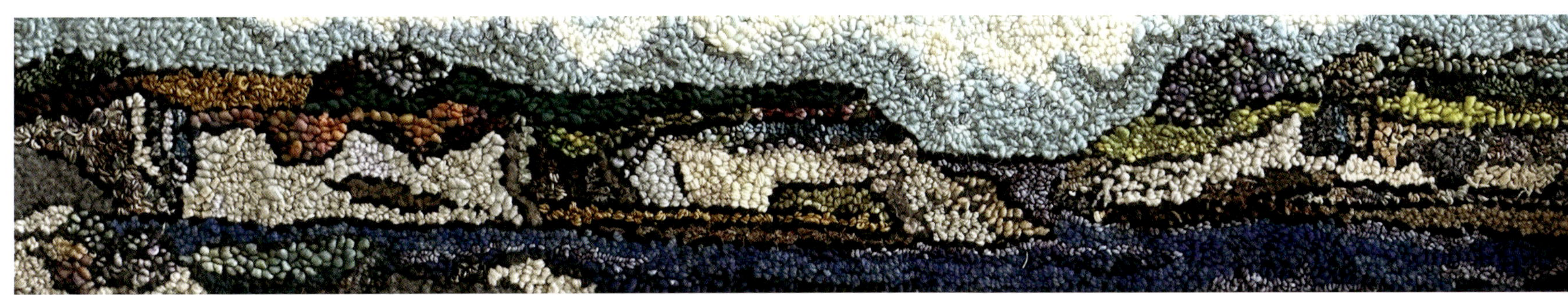

▲ *Eastern Cliffs*, 42" × 8" (106.68 × 20.32 cm). I like to experiment with different shapes of rugs and to veer away from the traditional rectangles often seen in art. Changing the shape of your rug allows you to show a different perspective of the same scene. Here I outlined every rock in the cliff, and the outlining itself became an essential part of the design of the rug.

In fact, in some recent landscape rugs I have been making, the outlining is the most important feature of the rug. I chose bulky ornate yarns; that is, yarns with a lot of color or texture to them, and I used them to outline the cliffs and rocky coasts in these slightly abstract sea scenes. I added a lot more outline than usual, outlining every crevice and rock in the hills, making the outline more predominant and a more important part of the design. These rugs are really all about the outline. Even when they were completed, the outlines did not recede and remained integral to the rug. It is the outline that makes these rugs stand out.

Other times when I sketch a rug pattern on canvas, I have some loose multiple lines like I would have in a sketchbook. I sometimes like to outline these lines to accent the rug. Rather than just outlining one line to hold the form, sometimes I like multiple sketchy lines to accent the artistic nature of the rug, and to give it a more painterly feeling. I might use several different yarns to emphasize this kind of outlining.

Outline was traditionally used to create form, and to offset one color from another. It has a simple and basic beginning. In my work, over time this has changed and developed. It really is one of the foundations of the way I design. I do not minimize its importance, because it is often the line in my rugs. Outline creates structure and perspective and leads the eye in art. It is not a secondary element, but a primary one in my rugs. I love the tradition of it in rug hooking, and I love the potential it has to elevate design. It is an important part of hooking rugs and can really help you show what it is you want to show in your work.

Using the Traditional Rule of Outlining in a Contemporary Way for Landscape

- **You do not have to outline everything in your rug. You can pick and choose what you want to outline.**
- **If outlining is going to be a predominant part of my landscape, I often hook the outline, first choosing the wool and color with intention so that it will work with the rug.**
- **Line is important in design, so when you outline, you are highlighting. Whatever you outline will be highlighted and appear more important in your rug.**
- **If everything is outlined, then nothing will be highlighted.**
- **Outlining everything can create an interesting stylized effect in a rug.**
- **Outlining is essentially drawing lines throughout your rug. You can use it to create style in your rugs.**
- **It is often taken for granted as a traditional technique, but it can be used in modern ways to create a contemporary or graphic-looking rug.**
- **The color of the outline does not have to be black. Choose colors that work with the rest of your rug.**
- **You do not have to use the same outline color throughout the rug. You can have gray in one area, black in another, and teal somewhere else.**
- **The more interesting the wool you use for your outline, the more interesting the line will be. Textured yarns can make great outlines and make things stand out.**
- **Outlines can be hooked loosely, skipping lots of holes to create a thin line that recedes.**
- **You can also hook your outline tightly so that the line will be thicker and stand out.**
- **The width of the yarn that you use will affect the strength of your line. A ¼-inch strip of cloth will stand out much more than a single-ply yarn. This will change your design.**
- **Your outline can be wiggly or straight, depending on the shape you want to convey.**
- **You do not have to do all your outlining at first; however, trying to outline something once it has been hooked makes it difficult to get the shape that you want.**
- **Using outline in new ways is a good way to create a contemporary effect in your landscape. Be inventive and experimental with it. Try new things.**

▲ *Cliffs and Water*, 37" × 36" (93.98 × 91.44 cm). This rug uses grays so nicely. Sometimes grays in the landscape dull down the rug too much, but here the soft pale blues of the sky seem to overtake the gray. I outlined the cliffs with a thick and fully textured yarn.

In this rug I relied heavily on outline to separate the areas of the cliffs and shore. In fact, I made the outline a really important part of the rug. Without this outline, the grays would just blend together, and you would lose the face of the cliff. Outlining in rug hooking lets us separate one area from another, especially when there is not a lot of contrast in color.

▲ *Mystery of the Fundy River*, 8" × 8" (20.32 × 20.32 cm). Sometimes you can do a lot in a small space. In these riverside fields, I have used a mixture of seven to ten greens of a similar color and texture. The curly boucle yarn stands out because all the other yarns are similar in texture.

05

PAINT WITH WOOL

A Painterly and Intuitive Approach to Rug Hooking

What is painterly style in rug hooking? It means that you are treating the wool like paint, as if you were using an artist's brush and are hooking with marks and strokes. It means your influence in how you treat the wool is coming more from looking at art, and the work of painters, than that of traditional rug hooking. A painterly style means you are painting with wool more than you are hooking outlines and filling in. It forgoes traditional rules of rug hooking and emphasizes blending colors and textures to create soft impressionistic shapes and lines.

You are hooking loosely with your wool and blending colors together side by side. That is, as you hook one color, you leave some spaces so that when you bring in your next color, you can hook right alongside it and into it, making the transition from one color to another appear seamless. It becomes difficult to tell where one color begins and another ends. They are blended together. Blending your wools is an essential technique in painterly hooking.

▲ *Look to the Mountains*, 8" × 8" (20.32 × 20.32 cm). The beauty in this rug is in the deep-gold foreground that leads you into the fields . The use of red hooked horizontally leads us into the mountains.

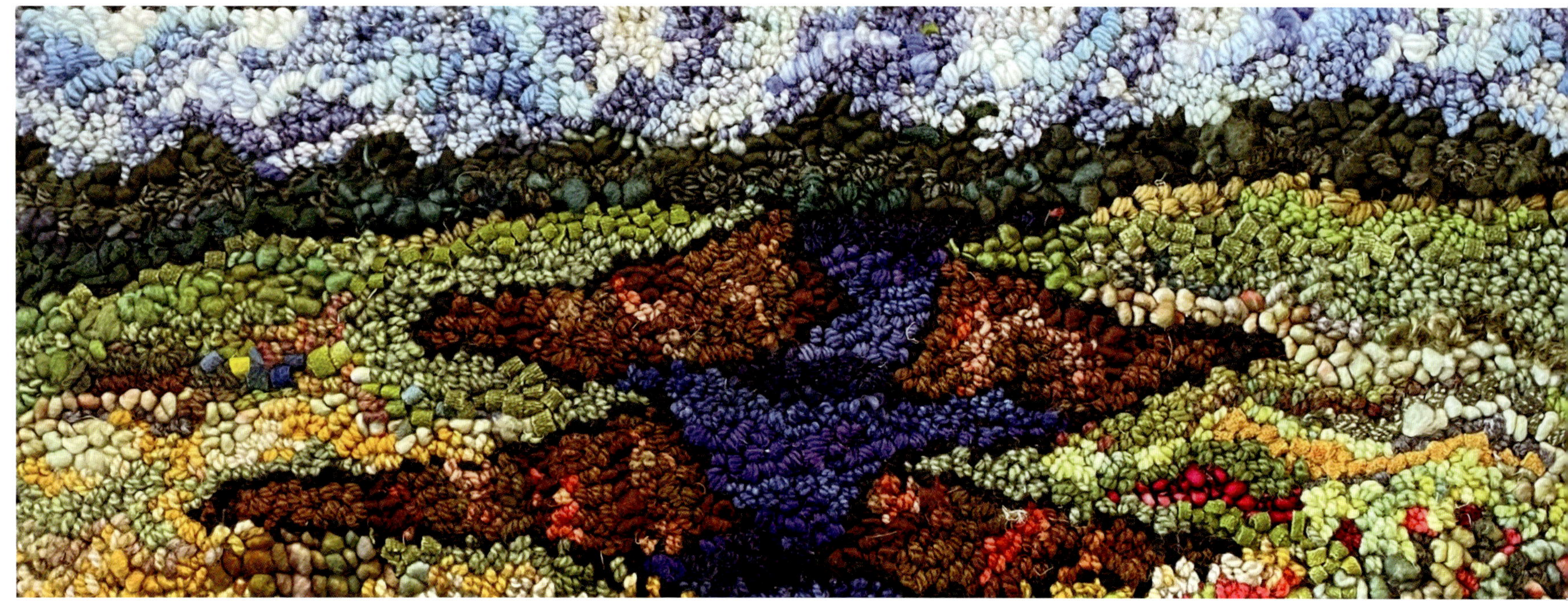

▲ *Love of Fundy*, 23" × 10" (58.42 × 25.4 cm). This beautiful, dramatic bay of water near where I live shows up in my rugs often. The landscape that surrounds you will seep into your work if you keep looking at it. Even in this small rug there is room to blend the colors in the field. One green changes into another seamlessly.

For me, a painterly style means I am relying less on the idea of outlining and filling in and looking at my canvas as a whole piece. Line remains important, but outlining is not the predominant thing that you notice in the rug. In a painterly style, one color moves into another color without a separation made by a line. And the emphasis is on blending colors that are in close relationship to each other. Simple dark lines can also be used to create separations or distinctions in the landscape, but they are generally not complete outlines. A painterly style is characterized by a looseness of movement rather than a rigid, grid-like style that has characterized some traditional rugs.

A painterly style is marked by soft edges and constant color transitions. It is more impressionistic than realistic. That is, the image is more an impression of what the artist sees than a perfect rendition of a photograph. The lines are slightly blurred, and the colors are often soft. It is about feeling, more than depicting.

I love this style of rug hooking in landscape because it is exactly the way the landscape feels to me when I look at it. The colors roll into one another; a field turns into a hill and meets the sky. It is the way I see the world, and often the way I hook it.

Blending the Wool in a Painterly Style

I think that learning how to blend your wool is one of the most important techniques in creating beautiful landscape rugs. You have to learn how to create seamless transitions from one wool to another, especially when they are similar in color. Once you learn this, you gain freedom of movement in your work. You will be able to make important transitions in color and texture. It is an important technique in hooking landscapes.

One of the mistakes I often see in landscape rugs is that the wool is lying side by side, one color almost layered on top of another color. The colors are distinct and form lines around each other. Each color is noticed for itself rather than as a community of colors. This can work in primitive rug hooking, but it interferes with a painterly style. I like to see my wools meet and give each other a quick kiss before going on their way. I want the wools to blend in and belong together in a way that suggests one would be lost without the other.

Hooking with wool is different than painting. In painting, you can change color and create light and depth with the layering of color. This is not true in rug hooking. We cannot layer wool on top of one another. Instead we must find a way to blend them seamlessly. In hooked rugs, color is not layered but laid side by side. I hook along, leaving spaces so that when I come in with my next color, I can fill it in and blend with the previous color. It is important how the colors meet. I want them to touch each other.

So here is the technique that I use, and **it is one of the most important techniques you will need** to practice to hook painterly landscapes.

When I hook, I leave some space and skip a few holes in the backing. I am not thinking about the holes in the backing as much as I am thinking about covering the surface.

I do not do this in a set pattern or a grid—that will not work. For example, you cannot skip every second or every third hole. You have to be random in your skipping of holes.

I hook loosely and skip holes and hook in curly or wiggled lines, depending on the effect I want to create, so that I leave room for another wool to come in alongside it.

Sometimes when I hook the second or third wool alongside the first, I dig in and hook it as close as I possibly can to the original color. Sometimes this even entails hooking every hole (this is sometimes called packing), so that you cannot really tell where one color begins or ends.

Essentially, one line or area of hooking becomes blended with another line of hooking, so that that become indistinguishable from each other.

You can do this with the same color or a similar color, or you can use a different color altogether to help you make a transition from one color to another in your landscape. For example, you might want to move from a field of yellow to purple, and this technique will work for that too.

Blending is important because not only does it allow for transition from one color to another in your rugs, but it lets us show light, movement, and depth with similar colors. It is the single most important thing I do in hooking landscapes. It allows me to move from a field of rose bushes to the green fields behind it without depending too heavily on a traditional outline.

In painterly rugs, I do sometimes use outline to distinguish one field from another and create depth. However, outlining is not always as important in a painterly style of creating landscapes as it is in some other rugs. I will hook big, long lines across the rug to show a sort of horizon line for a particular field. These lines are only sometimes black. Often I choose a deep, dark color such as brown, maroon, navy, or eggplant, depending on the tone of the rug. I will also sometimes stop the line before the edge of the mat, so that it does not go all the way across. And I often hook the outline quite loose, leaving room to blend it in as well. This keeps the outline from being too much of a separator, and more of a lead for the eye. When I hook above or below that outline, I will often blend the colors into the outline so it is not as distinguished.

Blending is easy on the eye and lets a person travel around the rug without being so heavily led by outlines. It allows us to show subtle changes in the land without an interruption. I rely on it heavily in all my work and am still working on my efforts to get better at it.

▲ ***Evergreens on the River***, 34" × 33" (116.84 × 93.98 cm). The crinkled lines leading out of the horizon and up into the sky gives me a feeling that there is something beyond my imagination. The lines are leading us away from the river and into the universe beyond it. How we hook our lines and in what direction can evoke mystery.

06

MAKING MARKS & SHOWING MOVEMENT

People are often daunted by the idea of making marks in their rug. Rug hookers have become used to hooking in lines or filling an object. But the idea of making marks is simple. It is similar to the idea that a painter uses different brushes to get different paint strokes. Marks are just the shape of the lines or areas that you hook in your rug. Most of us have a tendency toward certain shapes, lines, or areas as we hook. We often repeat these marks throughout our work.

I like to hook in all directions and have been heavily influenced by the brushstrokes of painters. I don't have to use a different hook to do this; I simply change the shapes of the lines and areas that I hook. Using different hooks might also change your marks slightly. I have used the same medium-sized hook for every rug I make. I like the feel of it in my hand and so never change my hook, but you could. I find that I have a selection of strokes or marks that I use again and again in my landscapes, and I have created a chart here to show you. This of course is not a perfect list. Sometimes I hook in random lines and patches as well, but I think it can give you an idea of how I use these marks to show movement in the landscape.

I am aware of the marks I make as I hook, and I find myself relying on certain ones. My challenge to myself as I hook is to be imaginative and change my most commonly used marks and even create new ones. I like to discover new ways of approaching my subjects, and creating new movements as I hook is one way of doing that. I try not to rely on the same marks for sky and sea over and over again. I like to be inventive and create new sources of movement in my rugs.

Instead of using different hooks to create different marks, the materials can make them unique. Different materials will make different marks or lines. So the same mark will look different with a big chunky soft merino wool than it will with cloth, or a fine worsted yarn. This of course means that each mark has many versions of itself, and also that there is a lot to discover about what a certain wool will do and what it is best for. Often, the material that you are using will determine the type of mark you make. It is very difficult to show a fine detail with a very thick yarn. For that, I will choose a thin yarn and hook it a bit closer together, skipping fewer holes.

Remember that you can change the shape of any of these lines or areas from vertical to horizontal or even put them on an angle to change the movement in the rug. You can also enlarge, reduce, or truncate them. It is important to modify them so you can emphasize what you need to show in your rug.

One of the most important things about creating marks is that they allow you to show movement in your landscapes. Movement is really about hooking different lines and shapes in your mat, so that your hooking is not too one-directional.

With good movement in our rug hooking, we can emphasize the shape of things and strengthen the images in our rugs. We create movement by hooking in the direction that makes sense for the area you are hooking. I like to hook hills with soft, wavy, downward lines, while I often use pointy upside-down triangles for my spruce tree. Different marks are used to create different elements of your landscape.

The marks I show in the chart are the ones I like to make. I bet you might already have some of your own. That's good. It will make your landscape rugs unique. Start noticing the ones you use and then make note of them. You could even make yourself a little sampler like I made myself here. Our lines and marks are a tool kit very similar to the strokes and brushes used by a painter. We need to get to know them and what they can do to use them well in our work.

And just like in painting, if we overuse one mark, using it everywhere in the rug, it will lose its emphasis and have a negative impact on the design and composition of the rug. I have done this when I paint and occasionally when I hook. Every element begins looking the same. You want to choose the right mark for each area of the mat. As I said earlier, you want to use the mark that makes sense and emulates the shape of the area you are hooking. When we choose different marks for different areas, it lets our eyes travel around the rug in a new way. The same mark used all over the rug gives a pattern, an almost dizzying effect, and you lose the individuality of the different parts of the rug. Changing the shape, style, and direction of your marks informs the viewer in the final piece, helping them distinguish one area of your mat from another, and contributing to the rug as a whole.

Marks I Use in Landscapes

01 **Straight line.** This is great for filling in areas, and hooking a house.

02 **Dotted line.** I simply hook a stitch on the line, the one below the line, and then back again. This just lets me create room for blending other colors as I hook the landscape. You can do this with a straight line or a curved line; it is a way of letting your rug hooking show movement and remain open to adding new colors.

03 **Heavy wavy line.** I often use this in the river, the sea, or water features in hooked rugs.

04 **Soft wavy line.** This line will show a lighter wave and less movement in your water.

05 **Small curlicue line.** I generally use this in my skies to show wind.

06 **Wavy vertical line.** This is often used in skies or hillsides to show that something is going down or up.

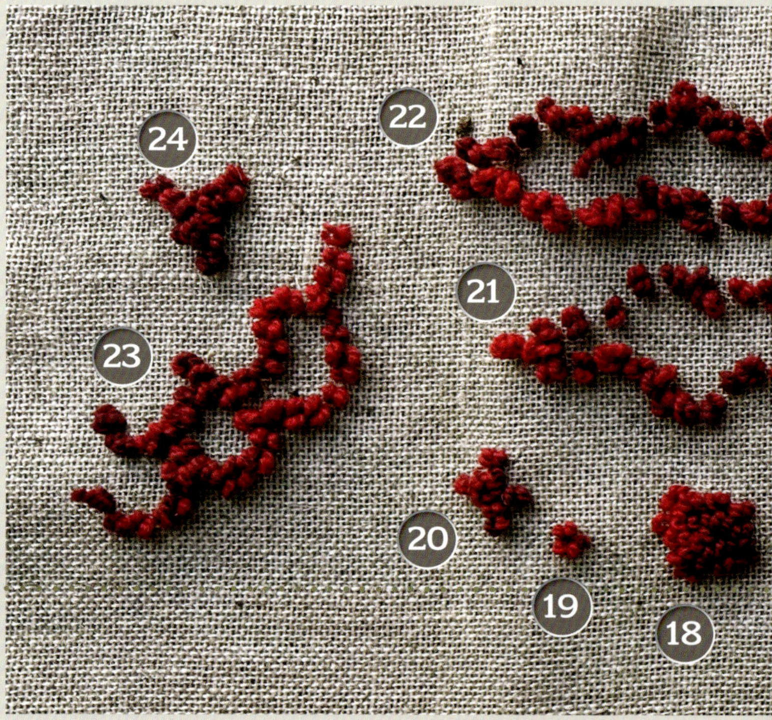

07 Big curlicue with sister line. This is used primarily in the sky, but sometimes in a big sea. I love the feeling of freedom and playfulness that it can add.

08 Landscape area mark. This is the kind of "patch" or area I often make to fill in the sea, the sky, or the water. Each time I make it, it is a little different, so that it does not become too matchy.

09 Stylized wave mark. I love this kind of line and how it symbolizes the sea.

10 – 15
Impressionist floral marks. I use these types of marks to create flowers in my impressionist garden rugs.

12 – 15
Stem lines. I use these marks to show stems of shrubs and bare bushes in my field rugs and abstract and impressionist florals.

16 Bumpy mark. I often hook this to fill in the sea, sky, or fields.

17 Thick patchy mark. Another useful mark for filling landscape, sea, or sky.

18 – 20
Big and little star marks. These are great marks to show stars, light, or movement in the sky.

21 – 22
Cloud marks. These are the shapes I often use to hook the clouds in the sky. I vary them all the time, so that they blend together. If you use the same cloud repeatedly, you will see the shape instead of the sky.

23 Bush lines. I like to use these to show that an area is a bush or sometimes, larger trees behind a house.

24 Upside-down V line. This is a great line to use repeatedly to show spruce or pine trees.

▲ I love these small hooked sketches of my walks. I like to hook them in small 8-by-8-inch squares and put them together as a collection to make one large impactful piece of art.

07

TINY LANDSCAPES

Bringing Together the Little Parts of Your World

Tiny landscapes are a beautiful way to capture moments in time. They hook up quickly, fit beautifully in a frame, and can be compiled together as a group over time. I absolutely love these little nature sketches. They are studies and practice for our bigger rugs, and I use them to work out larger ideas before beginning a big rug. I can work out colors and ideas in these small pieces. Often I am so inspired by a tiny landscape that was never intended to be a study that I decide to make it larger. They are a learning ground for you as you begin to hook rugs. I love hooking these and have been teaching others because it allows you to practice different subjects, wools, and colorways without overcommitting yourself. You can hook one in an afternoon and feel a great sense of accomplishment. There is nothing more inspiring than looking at a good finished rug and knowing that you have made it.

You do not have to hook a large rug to hook a fantastic landscape. When I began hooking small 8-by-8-inch landscapes, it was a hot summer, and I wanted to work small, so I began making these little squares. I loved the immediate gratification I got from them. I could hook one in a few hours. At first they were inspired by the summer countryside, or the beach. They were like little glimpses of nature that I captured in my mind during my walks.

Making Marks and Showing Movement in the Landscape

Since then, I have hooked hundreds of these little rugs. Sometimes they leave the studio on their own as one sweet little piece of art, and other times they leave as a family of nine, twelve, or even forty-nine little rugs that hang together. Individually, these rugs are separate little sketches hooked in a variety of wools.

The rugs, though they are small, can still hold and benefit from a large number of different wools. I have used up to forty different wools in these small rugs. When you hook small landscapes, you still need many wools, but you need only a little bit of each. So they are perfect for using up the wools we have left over from other projects. I always keep a basket of bits and pieces that I call my messy bits. For tiny landscapes, I always have this on the frame beside me, because I will often need just one 5-inch piece of a color.

Because I see each rug as a piece of art, I don't just rely on my leftovers. They are not only about using up the bits and pieces. I often select special yarns for each particular project. Usually I choose two or three colors to get me started, then I supplement with the little pieces left over from other projects.

▲ ***Forget-Me-Not***, 9" × 9" (22.86 × 22.86 cm). I love to make fields of flowers by hooking in dots of one color and surrounding it with another. Yellow and blue for forget-me-nots, red and black for poppies, yellow and white for daisies.

Forget-Me-Not

This little rug reminds me of playing in the ditch as a child and discovering the beautiful yellow center of the periwinkle-blue flower. It was my first encounter with my love for color.

For our purposes here, let's say 12-to-15-inch lengths of yarn or cloth. You do not have to have these exact yarns. Please substitute with what you have. It will make your rug more your own. For example, you could change the color of the flowers to cream or yellow for a completely different rug.

Forget me Not 8×8"

MATERIALS NEEDED

Sky

- 3 strips periwinkle-blue cloth
- 3 strips pale 2-ply turquoise yarn
- 10 strips of assorted sky-blue yarns
- 4 strips of very pale light blue for clouds

Trees

- 4 strands of worsted merino in a dark mossy green
- 2 strands of very dark 2-ply green

Below the Trees

- 6 strands of mottled turquoise yarn
- 2 strands of 1- or 2-ply variegated yarn with some mauve in it

Foreground Flowers and Grass

- 6 strips of gold or yellow for flower centers
- 15 strips of three shades of periwinkle blues; some can be cloth if you wish
- 4 strips of chunky, variegated moss green
- 6 strips of 2-ply pale green
- 2 strips of very pale light green
- 10 strips of pale to medium green in various colors and textures

You can start this rug by hooking up one or two loops for the centers of the flowers and then hooking the blue around them. I then hook the assorted greens around the flowers, accenting and reshaping the flowers as I do. Once the flowers are standing out, I add in the other greens to fill in the field.

I then begin my treeline and hook it in a wiggly line going up and down as I go across the rug. I use the mottled turquoise and the varigated mauve to accent it and meet the field of flowers.

Next, hook in your clouds in white or the palest blue and begin building your blue around them in curvy amoeba-like shapes. Voilà! Your field of flowers is hooked.

In these pieces, be mindful of the amount of texture you use, and do not put two or three textures too close together, since they can overwhelm the rug, and the details will get lost. It is the detail, the tiny bit of yellow in the left field or the bit of pink in the foreground, that give us perspective and balance. Think about how those tiny bits of wool that you hook in as details will appear in the rug. You need them to accent an area without standing out like a sore thumb. Accents should accent, not overpower. They are there to help us see something important as part of the bigger picture, but we still need to see the bigger picture.

Outlining in these rugs is used mainly for a few key features. There is not a lot of room, so I don't heavily outline, though I may choose a hill, rocks, or field that I want to stand out and then outline that. I tend to use a greater quantity of finer yarns in these rugs than chunky yarns, because chunky yarns take up too much room and can overwhelm the piece.

The most important thing that I try to impart in these landscapes is that they are just a suggestion of what is beyond them. I am giving a miniature picture of something bigger; there is more land beyond the square you are seeing. I do this by truncating fields, trees, or bushes to imply that they continue on beyond the picture you are seeing. I also sometimes extend the outline to the edge of the rug, and this brings the eye beyond the rug and makes the image feel more expansive.

Tiny landscapes are a great place to use the technique of hooking high and hooking low to give dimension to the piece. For example, when I hook a tree, bush, or flower, I might pull my loops a little higher and use a textured yarn. When I hook behind it, I will hook the negative space, that space around the object, a little lower and in a plainer yarn, such as two-ply worsted knitting yarn. This lets the object stand out and the background recede. This technique of hooking high and low is important in all landscapes because it lets us allow certain subjects to stand out more and others to slip away into the background.

The other important thing in these landscapes is not to get caught up in trying to show too much. I think of these as a glance of nature from my walk. It is a sketch, an impression of something I saw as I quickly walked by. So that is all I try to impart. I want them to be a quick reminder that the Queen Anne's lace was blooming, or the back field was full of clover. If I want to tell more of a story or show a lot of different details, I will hook a larger rug.

▶ *The Golden Season Triptych*. These three rugs with their daisies and goldenrod were created for a fall workshop in my studio. I wanted to capture that beautiful autumn light and the burnished nature of early fall.

▲ ***Fire Bush in the Field***, approx. 8″ × 23″ (20.32 × 58.42 cm). In our lower field there are red-stemmed bushes that stay colorful all year long. Sometimes they are the only bit of brightness in the whole field.

▼ ***Sudden Bloom***, 7″ × 18″ (17.78 × 45.72 cm). Framed bits of pink hooked onto a bare branch reminds you of the sudden shock of spring when you see the first blooms appear.

▲ *Little Yellow Flowers*, 6″ × 17″ (15.24 × 43.18 cm). Every summer the studio has a ten-minute-a-day challenge where rug hookers all over the world commit to hooking for ten minutes a day. This rug was one of the designs I created for the challenge so people would feel accomplished by hooking just a single flower.

▼ *New Harvest Moon*, 6″ × 17″ (15.24 × 43.18 cm). This is a kit design based on the blueberry fields of Cumberland County where I live. One of my favorite things is to see a day moon over the fields.

▲ *Spruce in the Pasture with Grey Fields*, 29" × 30" (73.66 × 76.2 cm). You'll notice that the trees in this field rug look quite different from each other because of the direction in which the branches are hooked. It is important to remember that the direction in which you hook matters.

08

MEET THE TREES

Hooking Trees, Bushes, and Natural Elements

Hooking Trees

I love trees. When I am around them, I think of how old they are and what they must have witnessed. I feel small in a forest with the trees towering above me, small but protected. I love the way the light shines through them, and how the moss glows underfoot. And because of this, I am drawn to hook them.

Trees are an important element in landscape. They are naturally part of many landscapes. They can also be symbolic in our landscape, representing strength, wisdom, growth, and many other things. A single tree has a stoicism about it, while a forest adds depth and meaning to our landscapes. I have often hooked rugs of seven trees, since I am one of seven sisters. So the number of trees you put in the landscape can also have meaning. Of course, depending on where we live, the trees we know will be different. I have grown up in a land of spruce, so this is the tree I most often use in my landscape. There are cedars that have framed our front yard for nearly a century, and we have an apple orchard. So the shapes of the trees in my rugs naturally reflect these trees.

I love to hook trees, but I often find them a challenge in the landscape. Once I add one, it becomes the center of attention, and I have to be careful of everything I hook around it. Yet, I am drawn to them because of the presence they add to an image and the meaning they can imbue in it. Practice trees on their own at first. Sketch them, then hook them as separate small rugs and get to know how to handle them, and then bring them into your landscapes.

The single tree is an iconic feature in landscape art. If you ask someone what their favourite tree is, they'll have an answer. It might change over the years, but you can be sure that they have taken notice of a lone tree somewhere that stands strong and stoic. My favorite is a big wild spruce that leans in the wind and hovers over a blueberry field on a high hill. Whenever I travel, whether it is down the road or to a another continent, I notice the trees. When I landed in Marseilles, France, I was so happy to see cypress trees in person. It was like meeting a friend that I had known only on zoom calls. There it was right in front of me.

When I see a single tree, I see strength and survival. When all else has gone, they are still there, on their own. The single tree is a symbol. Its shape and form are a perfect focal point in most landscapes. It is the thing that draws us into the picture. When I hook a single large tree, I really like to use a variety of dark greens, different weights and textures, and then I like to add a touch of teal, or brown, or plum. I sometimes outline the branches in a vivid color such as hot pink or red. This of course takes away some of the realism and adds a magic quality to the landscape.

▲ *Tree Portraits*, 32" × 12" (81.28 × 30.48 cm). I wanted a clear image of the kinds of trees that I most often use in my rugs. I created this rug so you could see my favorites.

Trees are often one of the first things we learned to draw as a child. Remember our little family portraits with our stick people, a house with a triangular roof, and a tree in the yard.

Trees can add balance in a rug or be a focal point simply by where we place it on the canvas. For example, a large tree in the foreground will be a definitive point of interest, possibly even a focal point. Two trees, one on either side of a house, will add an obvious sense of balance to a rug. I often use trees to create the design in my landscapes. They are great for adding pattern and repetition to a design. I also find that a row of small trees meeting the sky creates instant perspective in my rugs.

They can also add perspective to a piece by making them smaller or larger. A larger tree in the front shows us that we are close to subject, but a few smaller trees near the horizon gives us distance in a piece. Where you place your tree in your landscape builds the story of the place and shows the viewer whether your landscape is the view of a small garden or 100 or even 1,000 acres. Personally, I love a landscape with a single tree in the foreground. It gives the work a focal point and allows me to build a landscape around it.

I am partial to very dark greens when I hook trees; however, we can play with the color of trees, imbuing them with blue greens, lime green, or, truthfully, any color at all. When I hook a forest line at the back of my rugs, I use wines, teals, purples, navy, and black, to enhance various dark greens and give a separation between the little trees. This always looks good to me. I have not been as experimental with larger trees and have always leaned toward the dark spruce green of my childhood. I encourage you, though, to experiment with other colors and highlights.

Sometimes I outline the trees in my landscape, but often I do not. I do sometimes find it difficult to let the trees stand out on a landscape. There has to be a strong contrast between the color and the tree and the landscape behind it; otherwise the tree will blend into the landscape. I have made this mistake many times. I often play with the outlines of trees, adding reds, pinks, and oranges to outline them. This changes the nature of the rug, making it a tiny bit playful, or adds a sense of abstraction to it because it is not realistic. So this will not always work to separate the tree from its background. You can also outline the tree in a color very similar to the one you use in the body of the tree, and this will help emphasize its structure and can help it stand out from the background. You can also hook in an outline to add shape to the tree in a complementary or contrasting

▼ *Yellow House with Two Trees*, 32" × 12" (81.28 × 30.48 cm). This design of trees added to either side of a house feels stoic, even though the house is in a precarious situation. This deliberate use of balance implies a sense of symmetry and stability to an otherworldly image.

color, then remove it once the tree is hooked. This will help create form for the tree.

I also love a bare tree, with its big, dark branches sprawling. I find that dark colors such as black and navy work well for these because it is a color that stands out against everything. It also adds a dark, shadowy presence to the piece that is interesting, such as in my rug *Driving Through Maine*. I will often use several dark colors together to hook this type of tree, changing the colors somewhat randomly. The subtle changes in color add a bit of light and texture to the tree, especially from a distance. It is important because this takes away the flatness that would happen with a single dark shade.

Bushes

I have been teaching people how to hook bushes for a long time. One day I was teaching about the elements of the landscape to a group. I got out my hook and my frame and drew a little bush by the side of a house.

With my hook and some fleece, I began hooking the little bush. I was hooking it high and freely. As I did, I said, "Bush, bush, bush, that is what I am thinking as I hook this." A student named Nina excitedly said, "I got it."

A few years later, she said to me, "I think one of the most important lessons I ever learned in your classes was that day when you hooked a bush and said, 'Bush, bush, bush.'" I laughed because it seemed such a small thing to me, after all the classes she had been to. But what Nina learned that day was to be present to and focused on what you are hooking. Pay attention to the most important detail, thinking about what it is you are trying to make.

Bushes are quite simple to hook. I like to use fleece that is washed and dyed in shades of green. I am partial to brighter shades and a hint of lime for hooking bushes. Uncarded fleece is wool right off the sheep that has been washed but not combed out. When you're using this type of fleece, your bushes will appear rather wild and unmanaged. You can hook in bit of color in small shapes to create floral bushes. I like to use little rugged circles for roses, or small oddly shaped triangles for lilacs.

For years I have had a friendship with Delia Burge. Delia is one of the few farmers in North America who raises Wensleydale sheep. She is also a spinner, weaver, and knitter. She ran a gorgeous shop, Water Street Studio, for many years

◀ *Evening Beyond the Trees*, 20" × 13" (50.8 × 33.02 cm). The corals and yellows in this sky are an effective change from always relying on blues as the traditional sky color. When you start watching the sky, you soon see that blue is only one of many colors that live there.

in Pictou, a small Nova Scotia town. She loves her sheep, and each year after shearing, Delia dyes their long locks in every color of the wheel, but with an emphasis on blues and greens for the Nova Scotia landscape. I buy a lot of Delia's uncarded wool and use it mainly in the little bushes I put into my landscapes. (Though her wool is also great for hair, rough seas, and flower gardens. We will talk about using uncarded fleece in those parts of your designs too.)

If you don't want the curly, wild texture of natural fleece, you can use carded fleece. Carded fleece is natural fleece that has been combed but not spun into yarn. It is smoother and more even and is often dyed commercially or by independent dyers for spinning. Carded fleece is sometimes dyed a solid color. I prefer when it is hand-dyed in a more painterly way, with several shades in the same piece of wool. This lends itself to a more interesting variation of color for the bushes. When you

▼ *Driving Through Maine*, 25" × 19.25" (63.5 × 48.89 cm). As we move into more-populated areas, sometimes our landscapes are more about houses than trees and fields. I love these landscapes too.

▲ *Woods Above the Marsh*, 21" × 7" (107.95 × 63.5 cm). This rug uses fleece and a boucle-style yarn to create a forest in the background. These wools are pulled higher to create a sculptural quality to the woods.

use carded wool, your loops will be less wild, more rounded, and almost bubbly in texture.

Fleece is interesting because it is a material that can be controlled. When I hook with fleece, I often pull a little strand of it away from the lock that it came on, and almost hand-card it. It is tempting to hook the whole lock, but this will create heavy, bulky loops. Instead I pull the locks apart and create my own light, fluffy strands to hook. You can hook it wild and high. Often I pull it up to an inch high, knowing that the next loop I pull will pull it back down to half an inch. I hook fleece hard and fast when I want to emphasize it. I skip lots of holes, hooking in maybe every third hole, and this lets the fleece bloom and cover the surface. But you can also hook the fleece tight and low and get a completely different, almost bead- or pearl-like effect. When you hook the fleece tight and low, you will often see a sheen on the wool, depending on the sheep that it came from.

In my bushes I often will use a mixture of cloth strips and yarn with either carded or uncorked fleece, because I like how I can show movement with the cloth or yarn against the more natural, wilder texture that fleece adds. For example, I will begin by hooking the cloth in curly lines, almost like a bunch of C shapes, and establish a pattern of this in the bush. Then I will hook in the fleece around this. This establishes the shape of the bush and makes it a little less wild. It also creates some depth within the bush itself, because the cloth is often lower than the fleece, and of course the texture of it is in contrast to the fleece.

Natural fleece adds an interesting texture to our landscapes. Wherever we use it, whether it is in a bush or just as a line in a field, it draws in our eye and adds interest in the area. I do sometimes add a bit to a field to imply that there is some rough area there. You do have to manage it though. When it is overused in a rug or pulled up too thick, it can overwhelm the landscape. When it is used sparingly and carefully, it carries us into the natural world.

▲ ***Sable Island Horses***, 30" × 22" (76.2 × 55.88 cm). When I came back from Sable Island, I cut out templates of a few pictures of the horses that I had taken there and used them as stencils to create a mystical design with stylized waves and bird shapes as clouds.

Taking It In

When I was a child, I used to visit a woman named Mrs. Eileen to eat her cookies. She was in her sixties and I was about four years old. I would go up the road to her house off and on throughout my childhood and sit in her kitchen and talk. In her hall there was a poster that recounted the shipwrecks that happened on Sable Island. I was always curious and slightly fascinated about it. So recently, when my friend Stephanie invited me to visit Sable Island with her, I was enthralled with the idea. Only a few people get to go to Sable each year. It is a protected Canadian national park.

Sable Island is off the coast of Nova Scotia. It is famous for shipwrecks and its nearly five hundred wild horses. A sandbar in the middle of the Atlantic, Sable has only one tree. It is a tiny Scots pine that has lived in the sand for forty years. It is in fact a survivor. The Nova Scotia government planted over eighty thousand trees on the island, and only one has survived. It is a remote, austere, and beautiful place.

And at first glance beyond the horses and the Scots pine, it would seem that very little survives there. Yet, after being there only for the day, you discover a complex ecosystem that is ever changing with the wind, the sea, and, of course, the weather.

The horses can be quite gentle. It seems as if you could walk right up to many of them and rub your hands along their mane. They are protected, though, so you are not allowed. But you can sit and watch them from a short distance away. And I did sit quietly for long stretches throughout the day and watch them eat the grass, run, and play. And I studied the landscape, took a few pictures, and sketched a bit.

Mostly though, I just looked and tried to be present to the place. I wanted to see it through my own eyes and remember that. This is something very different than through the lens of a camera. Rather than spending the day taking pictures, I tried to spend the day really breathing in the salt air, listening to the sounds. The waves, the birds, the horses, the seals, the wind. These things have to be lived. Then I create rugs based on how I felt about it.

I spent my day on Sable wisely. I picked up shells and bits of leaf and seaweed and carried them around the island with me. I stared quietly at the horses, and I watched them running on the beach. I watched the waves wash over the big gray seals. There was a lot to see. Before I left, I put back all the bits of flotsam I had carried around for the day.

When we go places, and it does not have to be far or exotic, as long as we are present when we are there, we carry those places with us when we come home.

> "I wanted to see it through my own eyes and remember that."

▲ *Milkweed Field by the Pond*, 46" × 37" (116.84 × 93.98 cm). The deeper blues and the use of light mauves strengthen this sky, creating shadows and depth. The bits of red in the pods in the foreground contrast to the green grass and connect with the red in the blueberry fields beyond them.

09 KISS THE SKY

The Importance of Skies

When I wake in the morning, I go to my studio window and look beyond the tall spruce and hackmatacks at the end of the field and see what the sky looks like. This morning, in the big gusts of wind the clouds seemed like ships rolling by, their sails with silver linings and a bit of gold hidden in their masts. Other mornings I have seen deep pink or orange through the trees. I can tell you, though, it is never the same way twice. It is always worth a look. Making a practice of looking at the sky has built my imagination around it. It will build yours too. You will quickly see that it won't be conquered with a ball of pale-blue yarn. The sky wants to be seen. It is like the queen that watches over; she expects to be noticed.

Whenever you hook the sky, you are casting a shadow on the day in your landscape. Whatever colors and shades you use will tell us what kind of day it. So it adds a lot to the feeling of the rug. It tells us whether it is a cool winter evening or a sunny summer morning. The sky is part of the story of the landscape. It can be hooked realistically or magically. Magically means that I might hook flowers or seashells in the sky. Essentially, it means that I am not at all concerned with realism. I think of the sky as a vast space to create in. It is often a big space in the landscape rug where you can create feeling.

So I cannot tell you the color of your sky. You must look up over your own place in this world throughout the day and take note. And you must gather the wools that matter to your landscape. And you must must do this in August, and November, and January, and any other time of year, because the sky is always shifting. It is one of the most interesting elements in hooking the landscape, and it will matter in the rug a great deal.

When I look up at the sky, wool is not the first medium that comes to mind in re-creating it. The sky is ethereal. When I think of it, I think of opals, lots of shimmer, movement, and light. It seems better suited to watercolor, where you could create soft washes that fade into cream and gray. I began thinking about how I could do this with wool, and the most obvious way was to dye wool. I began to create light washes of dye on cloth or yarn.

I would dip the yarn in some blue dye and quickly use citric acid as a mordant to get the lightest blue and even leave some white in the yarn. These dyed yarns and cloth are often the main color in my landscape skies. They seem to give me a watercolor effect that I see in the sky when I look at it.

Creating interest in the mat is one of the most exciting things for me, and the sky is an important place to create interest in the rug. A few years ago at my sister's home for lunch one day, I picked up the paper napkin. It had a boat, the ocean, and the sky on it. The designer had used the sails of the boat, the sky, and the water as spaces to make more designs. It never fails to surprise me how design is everywhere, and inspiration is everywhere. I never expected to get a gobsmacking idea from a luncheon napkin, but then I remembered that the napkin started somewhere, in some artist's mind, as an idea, a drawing. Since then, I have been looking at the spaces that are created when I do my line drawings for my own designs. I now see these spaces as possible places for designs within designs. I saw the sky as a place to draw, a place to fill in. It is almost like scribbling on a whiteboard. There is opportunity in the sky to make a statement; it is a chance to tell people about the landscape you are hooking.

▼ *Two Icebergs*, 12" × 16" (30.48 × 40.64 cm). This is a great example of how color shows mood in a landscape. The whites and the cool pinks and the gray shacks all speak to the cold of winter.

Blue Skies Everywhere

The light is different everywhere. The world and our landscapes are always changing as we travel across them. Most of us, wherever we are, understand the idea of blue skies. We crave them, we stand under them thankfully, and we bask in their light. The old Irving Berlin song "Blue Skies from Now On" is imbued with meaning and hope, and we carry that blue-sky hope into our artwork. We begin with one loop, and we have faith that one loop will build upon another as we move toward completion.

Blue, though, in itself is infinite. It is not a simple color. There are so many shades of blue that can fill our skies. And so much swirl and direction we can create as we hook the sky. Our hook is like a pencil creating little line drawings within the sky areas of our rugs. Blue can turn to gray, to mauve, to cream. As our environment changes, so does the sky above us.

I like to think about the weather before I hook a sky because the weather affects the color of the sky. What is the day like? How does the color of the sky affect the color of everything underneath it? Once I was asked how do you hook fog. The answer is simply to makes sure that every color you use in your rug is grayed down a bit. If it is a bright-blue sky on a sunny day, you want more purity of each hue, and fewer grayed-down colors. The color of the sky determines the color of everything in the rug.

Once you choose the color, how do you decide what direction to hook the sky in? I have a big rule when hooking the sky. Avoid hooking straight across. In fact, it is one of the things that really bothers me when I see it in a hooked rug. When you hook the sky or any element of the landscape straight across, you see only the lines and lose sight of what you are trying to capture. The sky no longer looks like a sky; it looks like a flat prairie.

The sky is full of movement, so use movement in your hooking to get that feeling. You can draw swirling lines on your rug to guide you, or you can start by hooking those lines right in your sky as a guide. I like to choose blues, but don't underestimate the power of other colors to create mood, such as pale greens, mauves, pale yellows, and grays. These colors make blue even more blue and can really bring light into your sky.

You can learn how to hook the sky by looking at the work of oil painters and the shapes they used to create clouds. I still study these books today to get inspired when I hook the sky. Their brushstrokes can be approximated in wool with the hook. You can emulate these shapes in your skies.

I am often really liberal with creams and whites. Some days the sky has more cloud cover than blue. You can choose several shades and hook large cirrus or cumulus clouds. You can add natural or carded cream-colored fleece in your clouds to achieve a bit of a sculptural quality in the clouds. I love to hook the sky in big, swirling motions and create streaks of white or deeper blues to show movement. Create a little contrast in the sky to add some interest there. It is an important element of the landscape, and we want to bring people's imagination into the sky when they look at our rugs.

Looking into the Trees

Often I hook trees where my land meets the sky. And it is important when you hook the sky here that you maintain and enhance the shape of your trees. The tree itself is the positive space, and the sky behind it is the negative space. Both are important. Often, people hook around the trees, but when you do this, you are not really hooking the sky; instead, you are outlining your trees. Don't make this mistake. Instead, think of the area behind the trees as sky and hook it in continuous patches that go across the sky, and behind the trees.

Choose one to three colors to hook this area that contrast with the trees, and hook them in linear patches. Each sky color doesn't have to go all the way across the rug, but it is good to have some continuity with similar colors on either side of a tree. This helps create depth. Depth is achieved by the continuity of the sky colors behind the trees.

The colors used here could be slightly different than the main sky or the same. You can use a shade darker and get in between the layers of branches. Don't outline the tree branches, and make sure they are hooked in organic shapes. This means the sky behind them will also be hooked in an organic shape. Try not to tame the branches by hooking rigid little lines here.

You will have only small spaces to hook your sky in, but even three loops can be hooked in a wavy little area or line.

When the Storms Come Rolling In

Having grown up and lived all my life near the Atlantic Ocean, I have seen my share of storms, and I have drawn my own conclusions in my art about the colors of the storm and the shape of the wind. When I think of storms, my imagination goes straight to dark gray blues, aqua, cream, and of course gray itself. This is what I see. Since each of us knows a different climate and a different landscape, it is important to ask ourselves as individuals what we see when we think of a stormy sky. For me, this is the key to creating good landscapes: knowing your own feelings and beliefs about the land you are wanting to re-create.

A stormy sky is not just a gray sky; wild weather can be expressed in all kinds of ways. Think moodiness, swirls for wind, and let your imagination go with color. It can be made up of shades of grays and blues and creams with lots of motion and movement. I think of a stormy sky as one that is unsettled and has a lot of drama. You can use dark colors to emphasize the heaviness of the impending storm. Deep shades of gray, gray blue, and gray green really emphasize that heavy feeling. But dark green might be just the color you need to put the storm in your sky. Try not to limit yourself by your traditional view of what are stormy colors. Experiment and expand your stormy horizons.

Clouds in the stormy sky could be pale yellow or lightest gray or cream to accentuate that unsettled feeling, but again, you might want to try light teal or mauve.

Most stormy skies would have a lot of wind, so movement in these skies is important. Hooking big, circular, swirling lines in a color that is deeper or lighter than the rest of the sky will get this idea across.

Looking Up into the Night

When I pull into my driveway at night, I look up to see if the stars are out. These are really just little white, shiny dots above me. I translate it into wool, perhaps some bits of sari silk hooked in one or two loops surrounded by black yarn, and the cloth of an old navy wool skirt cut into strips. That is the simplest night sky I can imagine, and I have hooked it countless times. Sometimes I substitute the white dots for gold or yellow ones. This always looks good. If there is a house in the rug, I can put some yellow to fill in the windows, and that will look as if someone has their lights on. It works every time. And that is a simple night sky.

You can use a navy skirt as the base of the night sky and add two or three other similar, but slightly brighter, shades of navy with it. Throw in some black, dark green, or purple for highlights. Hook tiny circles of yellow or white, two or three loops each, for stars. You could also ask yourself what if my stars were orange or lime? What would this do to my night sky? Remember that color evokes feeling, and every time we change the colors in our night sky, we get the chance to change the feeling in our landscape.

You can add some multicolored yarns with red, pink, green, or lighter blue if you want some drama in the night sky. Little bits of color help enhance depth and movement in the sky.

I like to hook the sky from the ground toward the top of the sky in big, thick lines with a curve or a wave to them. I always start my lines and finish them in different places; this helps create movement. I like the feeling of movement coming from the ground up. You can also start at the top and come downward on an angle, circling your stars if you like. Like all hooking, there is no one way. The most important thing is to create movement, and this mainly means that you avoid hooking in straight vertical or horizontal lines.

▲ *Standing Under the Big Moon*, 31" × 17" (78.74 × 43.18 cm). This rug uses a lot of textured wools to add interest to the field. It is simply a single-line landscape created by adding a soft, curvy line just a few inches above the center of the rug. The moon creates a focal point.

When the Sky Is More than Blue

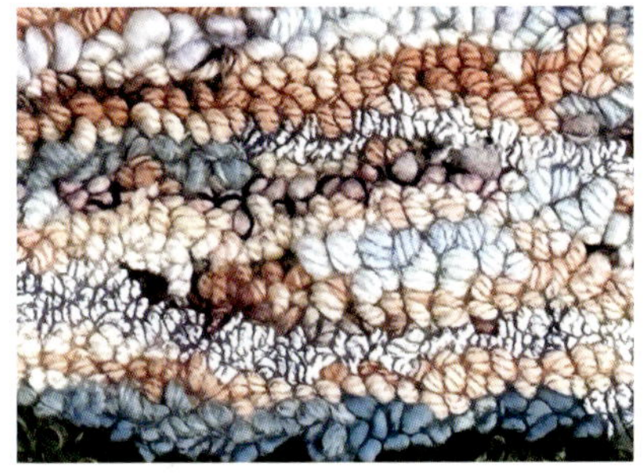

In seeing the sky as an area to decorate, I have had some fun creating skies in my landscapes with motifs in them. I have hooked flowers, paisleys, circles, squares, and diamonds, and I am open to playing with more motifs in the sky. This moves my landscapes away from realism toward a dreamscape, or invented landscape. It has a semiabstract effect on the rugs.

It can be seen as a simple decorative effect in rug making, but I really think of it as a way to be more expressive in my work. When I choose a motif, I usually draw them on first, making sure that some are truncated on the edges so it has a natural look. I don't want the daisies or paisleys to be perfectly centered and not reaching the edges of the sky. To create an all-over motif, it is important that they reach the edge of the area and not all be centrally located, since this affects the overall design. They should cover the entire area that you have chosen to create in the motif. I then hook each little item like they are separate work of art. Do not try to make each one exactly the same; they will be uninteresting. Just let your heart free and your hands play. They do not need to be the same. I like to draw the motifs freehand and have them all different shapes and sizes. You could create a template by drawing your motif on yardstick, cutting it out and tracing it.

I then contrast the color of the motifs to the background color of the sky. You can hook motifs in a stormy, sunny, or night sky. There is room for the imagination here. I sometimes use

▲ *Lone Sunset*, 12" × 31" (30.48 × 78.74 cm). Sometimes simplicity is best. After years of struggling with complicated ideas, using many colors for a sunset, one evening I landed on the idea of just adding pink to the lower part of the sky, and it worked. I did three small versions of it before I did the larger rug.

▲ *Lone Sunset 1*, 9" × 12" (22.86 × 30.48 cm)

▲ *Lone Sunset 2*, 9" × 12" (22.86 × 30.48 cm)

▲ *Lone Sunset 3*, 9" × 12" (22.86 × 30.48 cm)

different colors in each motif, feeling free from worry that they are all the same. I don't want that. What I do want, though, is for the motifs to relate to each other and create a semiconsistent pattern throughout the sky. These motifs create a sense a wonder in your landscape, as the sky is meant to do. Most of us look up at the sky and sense the mystery and the wonder of the world. When I put motifs in the sky, I am creating this sense of wonder in a simple but, I hope, profound way.

The Endless Sky

These are just a few ideas about how I hook skies. We know, though, that the sky is endless; it goes beyond what we can see or imagine, so I have just touched the surface. No book could ever do it justice. Each day I look at the sky, only to find out that I barely knew it at all before. Today, out my kitchen window as I boil lentils to make my husband's family's traditional lentil soup, the sky is a milky gray. It feels as if I have looked upon it a thousand times before, but I have not. It is new, a new morning, and the soft pale lines of silver that hit the tree are different than they were yesterday. And today will be different too. So my job is to watch the sky, to pay attention, and to pick out what is beautiful in each sky I stand under and in each day I walk through.

The Making of Sunset Cottages

Sometimes in late winter, when the light is lasting a little longer, I like to catch the last of it with a quick evening walk before supper. One evening I was lucky enough to catch the sunset painting the sky a pink touched with coral. It was there over my neighbors' small white bungalow, and it looked perfect. It was one of those evenings when you felt grateful to be witnessing the sky changing before your eyes.

I marvel at the ever-changing sky. That night, I came into my house and sketched the sky over the cottage three times. It is never the same way twice and changes minute to minute, so I decided to hook it three times, three versions of the same sunset.

I took two hand-dyed yarns in shades of coral and pink with cream, and I hooked lines across the whole sky area. I then chose four hand-dyed blues:

a pale, thin, dusty blue and white silk
a thick, three-ply, cool blue that was plush and soft
two gray-blue yarns

Neither of these yarns were exactly the color of the sky that evening. This is part of rug hooking. Wool holds color differently than the natural world. We are always approximating color when we hook. We just do our best imitation of what we see. I have learned to accept this and use colors that are close and feel like what I saw, rather than strive for a perfectionism that cannot be achieved. I make compromises, because otherwise I would be on a continual search for the right color.

I mixed the blues in, again hooking horizontally across the sky. And in each small rug, I mixed how I used the blues, so I would end up with three different studies of the sky (see them at left). A simple cottage was used as the focal point of each piece to lead us into the sky. I also varied where I placed the cottage in each rug, so I could get a slightly different perspective. This made sense to me as I had been walking, coming closer to the cottage as I walked toward it.

These three pieces are studies of a pink evening sky. Studies let us work out an idea in a small, quick way before we embark on a larger piece. I have struggled with sunset sky over the years in my rugs, never really feeling that I captured the beauty that emanates from the evening sky. So in simplifying it, I was able to play with this idea with more success, I think.

I then chose to make a larger piece of the Sunset Cottage. One rug often leads to another, and the little sunset trio made me want to hook it bigger, because bigger would give me more room to experiment in the sky. I also wanted to focus on the landscape, to make it more sweeping and show the isolation of the house. This allowed me to add two more variegated pinks. I was excited that I could push my sunset further and maybe bring my work to a new place. I like the challenge of going larger from a study and using the same technique of hooking linear, cirrus-shaped clouds to create a simple sunset. This idea worked well in the larger rug (page 78, top) also. I could have used just the two shades of pink and coral without the addition of the variegated yarns, and it would have been good, just less interesting. Highlighting with the new yarn gave the sky more interest and depth. I find that the small bits of interesting yarns add a lot to a rug. In this case, I used a multi pale pink yarn with a black thread through it, and another yarn with some purple in it. I did not need a lot of either, but together they gave more depth to the sky and made a more striking rug.

▲ *Fields near the Shore*, approx. 8" × 29" (20.3 × 73.7 cm). In this rug, you can see I am hooking horizontally and creating shapes and making marks that emphasize the width and expansiveness of the landscape. There are bits of velvet in the upper midfield. Once in a while, I will add details that are not wool.

▲ ***Tantramar Barns***, 29" × 55" (73.66 × 139.7 cm). Houses or barns can be repeated in a pattern to make the rug more of a dreamscape than a landscape. Notice how the gray in the foreground field and in the sky reflect upon each other. The yellow hooked into the sky gives it a meddlesome feeling, as if there might be a storm brewing.

The Marsh

The first time I came to Nova Scotia, we drove across the Tantramar Marsh, an enormous swath of lowland that separates Nova Scotia from New Brunswick in Eastern Canada. After driving through Spruce Forest, we came to a wide opening in the landscape. On either side of me were wide, flat fields of tan-colored land. The left was dotted with big gray barns in the distance. On the right I could see a muddy bay, which I would later learn was the famous Bay of Fundy.

I am embarrassed to say that at the time, it looked like a wasteland to me. I was a teenager. Biology was just a subject I had in school. I had no idea of the life that existed on the marsh. The birds, the insects, the grasses that made up a diverse ecosystem. It was just a place, and I was not crazy about the way it looked. For me it was as simple as that.

But here is the thing that I learned. And you probably know it too. You too have probably landed somewhere and felt like you did not belong. Sometimes we feel as if we are not part of a landscape. Sometimes it takes awhile to be in a place before you can love it. I have learned how a landscape grows on you. The one you live in and observe and pay attention to is the one you learn to love. When we remain in a place for a long time, we learn to appreciate the subtle qualities about it. We begin to see the beauty that is there because we are present to it. And that marsh has become part of home for me. After years of knowing it, I feel like we belong together, and I see its own particular beauty.

It is easy to quickly fall in love with bi,g majestic views and sweeping ocean scenes. These, though, are not everywhere. Most of us live in our own little place, if we are lucky enough to have one. And most of us live without incredible vistas. Most of us live in just a place. And that place is the place we come to love.

"We begin to see the beauty that is there because we are present to it."

▲ *Lupin Field*, 17" × 14" (43.18 × 35.56 cm). You can show a field of flowers by hooking a few shades of a single color right across a large area of the rug. The mauves in this field rug do just that, and they rise up to meet the houses. There is also a second planting of lupins at the bottom of the house.

10

PLANT THE WILDFLOWERS

Hooking Flowers and Gardens

I need to start here with complete honesty. I am not a gardener. The only successful gardens I have ever planted have been with wool, and they have grown into rugs. My experience with flowers is from admiring what is wild around me and what is in other people's gardens. Even in the heat of the summer, you are more likely to find me leaned over a rug-hooking frame than you are to catch me weeding a garden bed.

But I watch, and as you know by now, that is a major theme in this book. I am an observer. I look at a bed of flowers and of course I am taken by the fabulous colors, but what really captivates me is how the shapes of the flowers change when partially covered by a leaf or when they lean into each other. They morph into little amoebas comforted by each other. I like to peer into their centers and see the little abstract painting that is at the core of each one. The little stamen that gently reached up out of the flower intrigues me. There is a lot to see in a single bloom besides the color.

The color represents the immensity of the flower in rug hooking. It is the main thing that draws us in. Big, puffy geraniums made up of many tiny flowers gathered together are showy, but put some trailing lobelia in that pot and there is a sudden wow. You cannot take your eyes off it. And because we are making rugs, we can use color to show representations of flowers more easily than we can show the tiny details.

Color and basic shape are the two things that are most important in hooking flowers and gardens in this style of rug hooking. If we get tied up in the tiny details and try too hard to render the flower as perfectly as it appears in reality, we will lose perspective. You can add this kind of detail in a macro version of a flower, but for landscapes we are trying to simplify the flower and give an impressionistic view.

Impressionism originated in France in the late 1800s as a new way of painting that focused more on capturing the idea of something than representing it fully and accurately. One of the subjects was nature, and of course flowers. The effort among these painters was to capture the color and light of a moment in nature. You could see the artists' brushstrokes and relaxed approach to painting in the work. I think this movement has a lot to teach rug hookers. I like to look at landscape paintings of gardens and see how the painter gave me the impression of lavender or lily pads. I study the colors and the shapes they used to help me understand how they achieved a certain effect.

This study, of course, is ongoing and wide. Each artist approaches each flower and field differently. You can learn things from all periods in art history—things from Van Gogh that you will not learn from Monet, and vice versa. And our study can go beyond the most famous artists, to all the lesser known or even unknown painters who captured the landscape in this style. We might seek out the works of Paula Modersohn-Becker, an expressionist painter, or Berthe Morisot, an impressionist, to see how they approached landscape painting. We have so much to learn and they have so much to teach us. It is this study of painters that has made me any good at all at hooking flowers in the landscape.

▲ The Queen Anne's lace and tansy are hooked in the foreground to take center stage, and there is a myriad of golds and green behind them, with some black outlines that don't go right across the rug, to divide them and create a sense of distance.
Past August #1 *(left)*, 17" × 29" (43.18 × 73.66 cm) | ***Past August #2*** *(right)*, 17" × 29" (43.18 × 73.66 cm)

▲ *Beyond the Peonies*, 50" × 56" (127 × 142.24 cm). You can put a large element such as the peonies shown here across the foreground of your rug to show perspective and depth. The items behind it will appear in the distance.

The main thing I have learned is to simplify. This is so important in rug hooking. We are using fairly large pieces of yarn or cloth strips, and there is not enough room with the medium to be too attentive to fine detail. Instead I have focused on learning how to effectively get across the idea of something rather than the exact image of something. If you can accept this, then rug hooking is a good medium for you.

If I can capture the basic shape of the outline of the flower, it will help a great deal in getting my idea across. The more simple I can make the outside shape of the petals and the flower's center, the more it will look like the real thing when I hook it. I also have to draw what that flower looks like when it is crowded against another, or when a petal has fallen off, the bloom has wilted, or the flower next to it has died and is much darker. As I hook, I think about the stages of the flower's life. It is in that perfect full bloom for only a little while, much like humans themselves.

When I choose color for a flower, I tend to select three shades. The middle shade is often the one I like for the perfect bloom, with the lighter and darker shades for variations if there are many small flowers together in a garden. In a larger bloom, I will sometimes use the three colors as a way of shading that bloom.

Now, shading sounds difficult, but it does not need to be in rug hooking. You can simply bring your three colors together, making sure they are close to each other in shade, and pull them randomly to show a little light and movement. If the shades are close together, this will work fine, and you will get the feeling of a shaded flower without all the thinking about where the light falls. Trust me, this can work in impressionistic hooking. As you do this, after a few times you might become more sensitive

▶ *Hot Pink Garden*, 12" × 10" (30.48 × 25.4 cm). This will look like a mess of pinks while you are hooking it. But when you add the green and step back, you will see the flowers emerge. Sometimes you need to step back from your rug to see what is happening in it.

to the shades and where you put them. This random method is a good starting point, especially in small pieces.

When I choose my colors for flowers, I sometimes look to nature. Purple says iris, red says geranium, and yellow says goldenrod. When I want to get the idea of a specific flower across, I use the color of the flower. However, often I am looking at the garden that I am creating in the rug and I am choosing colors based on how they look together in the rug, and I am not thinking about realism at all. My shapes are not specific to a particular flower, and so the colors do not need to be either. I work from my imagination, and that gives me a lot of freedom in my color choices.

◀ *Path Through the Magnolias*, 44" × 47" (111.76 × 119.38 cm). Sometimes a rug is inspired by many places. This rug was inspired by the forest on my walks down a rural road and a magnolia tree outside a city apartment. We can bring them together in our imagination.

▲ ***Wild Rogues in the Garden***, 57" × 72" (144.78 × 182.88 cm). I have intentionally forgotten about perspective in this rug, where tall sunflowers shadow pine trees. I love how this adds drama and some confusion to this massive tangled garden.

▲ ***Waiting on the Northern Coast***, 26" × 31" (66.04 × 78.74 cm). An iceberg looms in the distance, while the sea is hooked full of fishlike shapes. The wind is created in the sky by hooking huge swirls and repeating this directional hooking all over the sky.

Leaving Home

I grew up in Freshwater, Placentia Bay, near Argentia, where the ferry runs between Newfoundland and Nova Scotia. Well, actually between Cape Breton and Newfoundland. When I was a child, my mother cleaned the ferry boats, and she loved that job. She would walk to the foot of the hill and get in the back of Jimmy Houlihan's van with eight other women, her friends mostly, and they'd drive down to the terminal and give the ferry a going-over before the next load of passengers got on again.

I used to dream about going on the ferry. My friend Brenda Duke and I, when we were in grade 6 or 7, used to plan a trip where we would ride the ferry over to North Sydney and just come back on it. We never even planned to get off the boat. I think we just wanted to say we had been somewhere. We wanted, I suppose, to see the world. And for us, the entry way to the world was Cape Breton.

When I finally did get on that ferry, it was with my father and mother. We had a cabin and had packed sandwiches and Ritz crackers, and I was so happy.

From that ferry trip I learned so much. I learned that the sea offshore is sometimes more green than blue. I remember the moment I learned that, talking to my father looking over the rail. I can still see the aqua swirl tangled with foam over the side of the boat.

I learned that you don't have to go very far to see a lot. And I still believe that today. Some people can go to Nepal and not get as good a story as if they had gone 10 miles down the road. And that, I suppose, is because we carry ourselves with us wherever we are, and our stories live in us, and if we recognize that, we can find a good one anywhere.

And from that trip I learned that Nova Scotia is a beautiful place. It is lush, with good green earth, and I learned that there was beauty everywhere, different kinds of beauty wherever you go.

When I go out the door, I am surrounded by trees and water, and skies that change from one minute to the next. So how can I not be a rug hooker? Every time I turn around, there is inspiration raining down on me, and it is all because I live here.

And it is because I have memory. Memory of ordinary days watching cars go up the hill, of evenings drinking a beer while looking over black rocks covered in barnacles, memories of sisters dancing in the living room. When we hook rugs we have both: We have what is right in front of our eyes at any given moment, but we also have the past, our memories.

And we hook rugs to capture it, to re-create it.

Here in Nova Scotia, rug hooking is a big part of our culture. It is something that our families, our mothers and grandmothers, have been doing for generations. It is a way of recording our culture, and our rugs help us hang on to our landscape and our changing places. No matter where we are from, we have culture to record, and we can do that in our rugs.

"I learned that you don't have to go very far to see a lot."

▲ ***Light Lifting on the Water***, 32" × 18" (81.28 × 45.72 cm). Sometimes there is a lot of contrast between your sky and water, but sometimes, like in this rug, the shades are very similar. When the shades are similar, you need a horizon, trees, or, like in this rug, some mountains to separate them.

11

SETTLE BY THE SEA

Hooking Coastal Scenes

When you watch the sea, you know it can go from a calm, flat bay to wild, windy waves. When you live on the sea, you know that it is powerful, temperamental, and moody. The wind will change everything about it at a moment's notice.

Like so many people, I like being by the water. It settles me and reminds me of the infinity of the world. It makes me see myself for the small little soul that I am. I walk on the beach and listen to the waves and feel the comfort of just being, being enough. So many of us love the sea, and it is natural we would want to re-create it.

When you hook the sea, the first thing to decide is the mood of the sea. And this of course decides the mood of the rug. Is it calm and welcoming, or is it a deep, rough, cold, wavy water? This is your most important decision. What kind of sea do you want in the rug. From there you can decide the motion you want to hook it in and, of course, the colors. We cannot assume the ocean is blue.

Blue remains my main color when I hook the ocean, but I imbue it with shades of green or purple or add some black or wine if I want to. Don't limit yourself, because there is room for any color in something so vast and so deep. When you choose your colors, always remember that you are choosing the mood of the sea. The colors you choose imply the weather of the day, and the state of the sea. You could use dark navy to imply depth. Sketch in white or creamy-yellow waves to rough up the ocean and show wind. For a gray day, try adding in some gray blues or bits of dull aqua. You can choose colors that have a graying cast to them. A sparkling sea on a sunny day needs royal blue and perhaps a bit of wool with a sparkle in it. Sometimes you might add teal, purple or turquoise just to add some interest to your waters.

Don't limit yourself to blue or to the colors that I typically use. Start watching the water near where you live, or in books and on television. Take notice and you will find that your idea about the sea expands. I hook the sea that I see in my mind, and that has been influenced by what I grew up with and what I know and mostly how I see it. You will and you should see it differently. How we see things is what makes our work our own. This goes for all elements of the landscape.

My lines to hook the sea are soft, wavy lines hooked horizontally. I start by choosing a single color that is significantly or slightly lighter or darker than the other colors I plan to use. If there is a dramatic difference in color, the water can appear rougher. I then hook slightly wavy lines all over the sea, as if these lines were the waves themselves. You can increase or decrease how wavy your lines are if you want more or less movement. You could use white if you wanted to show that they were indeed waves, and this would imply a rough sea. I move these lines all around the area of the rug that is water. This technique lets me set a foundation of movement in the water.

After these are done, I will often choose another color and underline some of the first waves I hooked, and I will extend these second lines beyond the top line. In some cases I will hook these bottom lines double wide so that the sea does not become too linear. Hooking two lines ends up looking like areas rather than lines, and the water becomes more natural. I am always careful not to let my hooking become too linear even in wavy lines. In rug hooking, if the lines are too linear—that is, if you can see the lines of the hooking really clearly—when the rug is completed, you won't see the image as whole; instead, the view

▶ *Golden Field Under a Blue Sky*, 12.5" × 13.5" (31.75 × 34.29 cm). A single color, gold, is used in about ten to twelve different shades and textures to create this field of goldenrod. You can use single-ply, two-ply, and chunky yarns together in various shades of the same color to create a field of flowers.

Creating Mixes

Creating ocean mixes is a great activity to learn how to put different combinations together to hook a sea without actually hooking it. Take all your wools out that you find relevant to hooking a sea, and start putting together combinations that might work. When I do this, I balance out the wools—I don't just put equal amounts of each color in the mix. For example, if the sea was going to be mostly royal blue, when I create the mix I add mostly royal, then put in the other colors (teal and many others) in the ratio that I would use them if I were hooking the sea. This practice gets us comfortable and familiar with color. As well, it makes us aware of the colors we have in our stash. It is easy to forget that we have that periwinkle in the bottom of the basket. I use this idea of creating mixes for fields, hills, trees, and sky, and it can be used for all elements of the landscape.

will be distracted by the clarity of the lines. In my rugs, I want you to see the image more than I want you to see the motion of my hooking. I want the motion or direction of the hooking to be lost in the image.

Once I have underlined the initial wavy lines in some area, I will choose the main color I have chosen for the sea. I often call this the body color. Sometimes the body color is made up of two or three shades of the same color that are fairly close together. This gives me the chance to show a bit of light and reflection. I will start hooking one of the colors under one of my waves in a wavy line, but after ten to fifteen loops I will start hooking it up and down and then across. I will do this all around the water area, changing the main shade slightly with one of the body colors I have chosen. Essentially I am hooking big, thick, wavy areas rather than lines. And I use these areas to bring the initial lines together. When I hook these big, wavy areas, I fill in the spaces between my initial wavy lines and they become connected. At this point, I will often bring in an additional color that is similar and works with the colors I have chosen. This method means that I am hooking all over the water area and not from top to bottom or left to right.

▼ *Child Who Lives in the White House*, 20" × 14" (50.8 × 35.56 cm). This is what I would call a dreamscape, a place that lives in the imagination more than real life. In rugs, we can create beautiful landscapes that reflect what we love.

◀ *Golden Point*, 17" × 12" (43.18 × 30.48 cm). In this rug, the seasons are brought together, summer and fall together. You can see how the use of textured yarn and the wavy lines gives this sea so much movement.

▲ ***Village on the Wavy Sea***, 48" × 48" (121.92 × 121.92 cm). Sometimes the sea is the focus. All the houses surrounded it and are there in that place because of the sea. The wavy curls reinforce the importance of the sea in this village rug.

▲ *Beach Roses*, 7.5″ × 29″ (19.05 × 73.66 cm). A straight line across the horizon contrasts with the bounty and fullness of the organic shapes of the rose bushes in the foreground.

This is very important for two reasons. First, it shows movement and energy. Second, it means that if I run out of a particular color, I can always blend in another, similar color to finish the area. I hook like this for background as well, or any large area where I need a lot of a similar color. So often I have seen people who begin an area in a solid color left to right and get to the last 3 or 4 square inches and run out of that color and not be able to match it. You do not want this to happen in your water or any area of any rug.

Mixing and blending colors is important because it allows us reactivity in our work. Suddenly it is more about painting than outlining and filling in. We can express the action in the water. We can show where the light is hitting the sea. We are going beyond a paint-by-number approach and approaching a more creative way of painting, and we do this with our lines and marks and our color choices. We are given the freedom to explore.

As with the sky, I also use the sea as a bit of a playground when I hook. You could sometimes hook paisleys in it or tidal pool circles and ovals in a decorative way, using the same techniques we talked about using in the sky. For years, my favorite way to add a bit of abstraction has been to hook oversized decorative waves. Often these are right in the foreground of the rug, and they change the rug from being realistic to being more of a fantasy or dreamscape. You could outline these waves in several colors so that they stand out and become decorative. These waves are a statement about the importance of the sea, both in the rug and in our lives. They take the rug to a different place. I sometimes even hook a wave in the foreground of a rug when there is no actual sea in the image. This to me is a symbol of sorts of the meaning of the sea in the lives of people where I come from. Perhaps we might not live right upon it, but we know it and we belong to it. It is part of our lives, our heritage and culture. Symbolism is an important element in designing and creating hooked rugs.

At times I have hooked large jumping fish, or net needles (a hand-carved wooden needle that was used by a fisherman to crochet nets), in the foreground of the sea. You could hook sea shells, or kelp, or whatever symbolized the sea for you in your ocean foreground, knowing of course that this will abstract your landscape. This is one of the beauties of hooked rugs, that there is no strong tradition of perspective in them. You can do what you like. The shell in the foreground can be larger than the house on the edge of the ocean if you want. By using symbolism, and being free and creative with our landscape design, we can pour our own stories out onto the canvas.

▼ ***Late Summer Promise***, 7″ × 18″ (17.78 × 45.72 cm). The warm golds tell us the season is changing, but the bits of pink and red in the lower right corner inform us that it is not quite autumn yet. Sometimes the colors we use tell the story of the rug.

▲ *Joy on the Horizon*, 23.25" × 17.5" (81.28 × 45.72 cm). A simple way of showing a sunset is to add a stylistic sun peeking over the horizon line. This rug is a magical place with women riding the waves of life.

▲ *Cold Blue Sea*, 12" × 13" (30.48 × 33.02 cm). This abstract landscape uses curly locks, a boucle yarn in the foreground, and this adds a sharpness to the icy rocks. You can use heavily textured yarns to bring attention and focus to certain areas of your rug.

▲ *The Rolling Sea*, 32" × 9" (81.28 × 22.86 cm). The use of thick and heavy lighter yarns in the foreground waves in this rug shows that the water is rough and rugged.

In Your Own Little Yard

You don't have to go far to study the landscape. Just out your door is far enough. You could create a whole series of rugs based on even a small patch of grass. The key is found in being there, really being there. When we observe and study what's around us, even the minutiae, our work can expand. Design possibilities become endless. The struggle becomes not what to hook but what to choose to hook.

There is beauty everywhere, so of course there is beauty at home. And we sometimes forget about it. It can even become mundane to us after seeing it time and time again. Taking in the world that surrounds us so closely is a practice, and you have to do it with intentionality. These are two different things. To observe is to see, but to really notice is to think of it, why it matters, and to find a way to remember. It is easy to forget the tiny miracles that nature brings to us. As I wander around my yard, I look at the seedpods and notice how they are different in every season. I look at branches, and I notice which are bare and which are full of blossoms. There is always something new to notice. I like to pay attention because the forms and shapes can become important elements in my landscape rugs.

Although, as I've mentioned, I try to leave my camera behind, sometimes I do take it out into the yard just to try to capture something in a new way. Looking through a lens in a familiar place can be like looking at it with different eyes. I also like how I can get macro views or truncate part of something through the lens. It can be helpful in seeing perspective and understanding design.

It is not easy to stay curious when you are seeing the same things every day. The trick is to go beneath the surface, to go deep rather than go wide. It is the work of an artist, the work of creating. We must know what we have if we are going to try to speak about it with our hands. Searching for the miraculous in the everyday is our work.

> "To observe is to see, but to really notice is to think of it, why it matters."

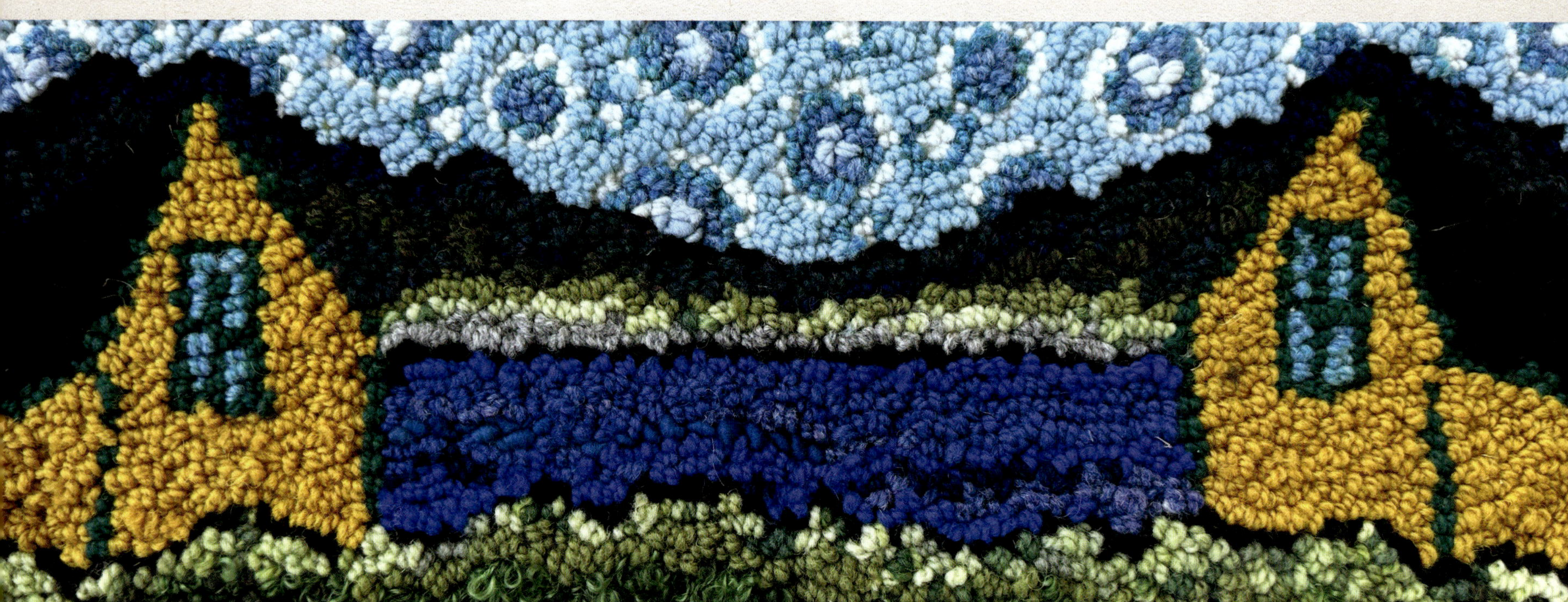

▲ ***Sisters on the Sea***, 6" × 17" (15.24 × 43.18 cm). My father's old friend lived in a gold house with dark-green trim and a green storm door. This is the traditional color of dory boats in Newfoundland and has become a favorite color of mine to hook houses in. In this rug, using the color twice and hooking the houses in a symmetrical way, directly across from one another, creates a familial relationship between the houses. I enjoy playing with landscapes like this and showing the warmth, and sometimes the distance that lies between the inhabitants.

12

BUILD A HOME

Hooking Structures

I love to look at a landscape with a single tree, or a bunch of bramble that looks as if no one has ever stepped there before. I also love the landscapes that have been layered with structures—those landscapes that humans have made their mark on and built barns, sheds, houses, and all sorts of other buildings. It is a mark that we have been there and claimed it at least for a time. Sometimes it is a new house perched nicely on a cliff, but for me it is mostly the houses that have been there for generations. The structures change the feeling of the landscapes. Suddenly they are less about the lay of the land and more about the people who live on it. As soon as you put a building on the landscape, you begin to tell a human story. It is a story about community and settlement, and always about love and joy as well as loss and malcontent.

Houses and buildings populate the landscape and lead us not only down paths and into hills and vales but into peoples lives. Structures are a symbol of the people who habitate within them, and for this reason I love to add them to my landscape rugs. They add story to beauty, and together these two things have marked may rugs since I began making them.

I began hooking landscape rugs with houses within a year of learning to hook rugs. It was one of the first styles of rug I was attracted to making. I grew up in a little place called Freshwater, where one house was built almost upon another. We had tiny postage stamp yards with little fences and gates that people crisscrossed as they liked. We lived almost upon one another. When I looked down over the hill, there were little square houses with triangular roofs, two-story flattop saltboxes, and the scattered modern bungalow before a big gray-blue bay. This view comes up again and again in my work. There will be different houses, different places, but it is a composition I am familiar and comfortable with.

Houses let us restructure the composition of the landscape. They give a starting point at times. Other times they give us a focal point. They let us populate and place and change the way we see it and the way it is seen. When you hook houses in your landscapes, the whole color palette changes. Suddenly yellow is not just for little flowers. It might be the main color in the whole rug. It also lets you introduce colors that are not naturally found in the landscape.

▲ ***House on the Cliff***, each 9″ × 13″ (22.86 × 33.02 cm). These landscapes are really about solitude. The single house perched on a cliff looks a bit like the interior of the earth. I like the use of outline in the cliffs to distinguish the rock. It is decorative and functional.

Colors for Buildings

Every time you hook a house in the landscape, you can think of it as painting your own little house. Simply outline the trim in one color and fill the body in with another color. Use your favorite color combinations. Dark green and dory gold, red and white, red and coral, white and turquoise are some of mine, but truly, I love hooking houses because the color combinations are endless.

You can outline each window in the trim color, leaving room inside them to add a tiny bit of gray tweed or sparkle, or something particularly special for the windowpane. A rug hooker once said to me that the windows are like the eyes of the house. I saw what she meant. It would be so easy just to fill in the tiny panes of glass without thinking, just to distinguish it from the rest of the house. This of course is a mistake. The windowpanes add light and interest to the structure. They are a chance to imbue the house with a bit of personality. Over the years I have made windows stained glass or, in larger houses, actually hooked people looking out the window. I spent my childhood looking out the window, so this is particularly comfortable. Other times I add color to the windows that will relate to the landscape around them, as if they were reflecting back the world they inhabit.

When you hook the outline of the house, you can hook it fairly tight and in a yarn that is a bit thicker, so the outline trim

color will not recede too much. When you hook the peak in a roof, you will want it to be really pointy, so hooking it tight and barley skipping any holes in important. You want to use your outline to really form the shape of your house.

Sometimes you might choose to add a third color as a trim and top of the windows or to paint the door. These would be the fancy houses, or painted ladies. You can add as many colors as you like to your structures. For me, though, it is most often two simple colors. I do not tend to hook elaborate or Victorian structures. I like the simple boxlike structures like the one I live in. Essentially they are a square with a triangle on top. When you look at a house like this as a series of shapes, it is much easier to draw them and add them to your rugs. They are the simplest things to hook; they just want you to take over the lead and be daring with color. They are best when they are layered upon one another and relate to each other if you want to show community.

When you start adding many houses, the landscape recedes and the community becomes the primary focus. Roofs are typically hooked in dark colors such as eggplant, black, dark gray. I have always loved a recycled dark tweed or plaid cloth cut into strips for a roof, though a dark-gray heather or tweed yarn can work as well. Over the years, I have taught many people to hook houses in their landscapes. So many have made the same mistake in outlining, or painting the trim of their house. They often outline the house, the windows, and the doors perfectly and then they proceed to outline the roof. They hook a line right across the roof, where it meets the sky. When this mistake occurs, I always ask them, "If you were painting your house in real lie, would you get up on the roof and paint a line of the trim color across it?" The response is always laughter, tinged with a bit of self-frustration. This mistake arises because they are thinking about following instructions rather than thinking about what a house really looks like. They are not in the village; they are not painting their own house. Instead they are focused on the mechanics of making rather than the imagination of making.

Try to be in the place you imagine the house to be when you are hooking houses in the landscape. Try to imagine how the ground meets your own house, how the neighbor's house is situated and sits upon the land. For example, I never hook the bottom of the house trim across where the land meets it. Instead, you can let the land rise up to meet the house. You can create a planting there and hook a little bush or flowers. You can think of it as if you were landscaping. You can plant a tree, add a bush, build a fence, hang a wash, and add anything that you think might add life to the village.

When you are hooking houses, you are designing, thinking about how the whole neighborhood will look, about what the color of one house will look like next to another. This is such a

▼ *Driving Through Maine*, 25" × 19" (63.5 × 48.26 cm). At times, like in this rug, the houses take over the landscape and become the landscape. We see a tall winter tree overshadow the houses, and aside from that, the remaining nature is a bit of grass that the homes are built upon.

◀ ***Between Two Places***, 36" × 36" (91.44 × 91.44 cm). This rug is a story about two landscapes that I love: Nova Scotia, where I reside, and Newfoundland, where I grew up. We can use a landscape rug to tell a story.

This rug was the basis for an entire show of my work called "The Very Mention of Home," which was exhibited at The Art Gallery of Nova Scotia for five years as part of their permanent collection.

fun, powerful idea. You get to build the community, creating the village as you would love it to be. This of course never happens in real life. Everyone has their own whim and will and can do as they like. Instead of a village of colorful houses, many communities are covered in white and tan vinyl siding. My village landscapes do not have to reflect the real world; instead, they reflect the world of our dreams.

I do sometimes, though, love to hook a solitary house, just as I love a solitary tree. They then tell a totally different story, and the landscape around it remains a primary focus. This is often the story of the introvert's or a lone person's relationship with the landscape around them. Many of us choose to live in a certain landscape. I know that I have a deep relationship not only with the land I live on but with the whole Chignecto Isthmus where I live. My relationship with the Newfoundland landscape where I grew up also runs in my veins. I love the rugged sea and rocks, and they feel like part of me. When I hook a solitary house, it is often like a kind of self-portrait, with the house representing me, of course. In these rugs, I am able to fully show the details of the earth, the moss, the rocks, the little bits of color that enliven the grass, and I love this. A single dwelling leaves room for the grass to grow and the land to take center stage, so I love hooking these rugs.

◀ ***Poppies and the Yellow Jacket***, 16" × 28" (40.64 × 71.12 cm). This is a playful rug. Notice the details of dandelions in the front and how the oversized poppies are in the shadows behind the woman. The rug is as much about the ground she is standing on as it is about her.

13

BE IN THIS PLACE

Adding Simple Portraiture

Sometimes I add figures to my landscape. When we add houses or people to our landscape design, these things become the focal point. If we look at a wide expanse of land and see a house or person, our eye is naturally drawn to that. It is a definitive point of interest.

I like to hook simple portraits standing before the landscape. I see these images as if someone was having their picture taken before a beautiful view. Most often, my people are women standing alone, a single solitary figure. This is a signature in my work. The person is in stark contrast to the land and is most often standing in the foreground.

If I delve into this idea, I could make all kinds of psychological assumptions about solitude and isolation. I more often hook women than men because I find the female form and their way of dressing more interesting. I sometimes wonder if this is a result of having grown up the youngest of seven sisters. As I child, I watched those sisters with curiosity and awe as they readied for church, for dances, and for work. To me, they were ever interesting, and as a small child at home I was in the position of observer while they were out in the world. Good practice for the artist that I came to be.

▶ *Holding Things Over Your Head*, 12" × 17" (30.48 × 43.18 cm). Sometimes your rug can be a very personal story. I am a homebody and, as I told you, I love where I reside. Once I managed to stay away from my house for sixty days, and I made this rug as a reminder that I can do whatever I need to do.

▲ *Cardinal in My Palm*, 11" × 17" (27.94 × 43.18 cm). Though a person in a rug becomes the focal point, you can bring the viewer's attention to something like the cardinal through the title of your rug. Notice the curls and rounded shapes of the hooking in the bushes and the sky.

Recently I was interviewed for a magazine article, and the writer said that when you hooked people years ago, they were always in large groups, and now they are often a single figure. She asked me what I thought about that, and of course it got me wondering. The truth is that as someone who hooks rugs and writes books, I spend many hours alone and in solitude, which is an important aspect of my work. Just as easily, though, these images could be about simplicity. I love the freedom that the solitary figure implies and how they contrast with the landscape. I do not have a definitive story, because that story changes from week to week, from rug to rug, like the story of our lives.

People and the natural world are two things I love in my life, so it makes sense that they would come together in my work. Before I became an artist, I had studied counseling and had planned to be a therapist. I wanted to help people make sense of themselves and their lives. I have always loved art with figures in them, though have found that most artists do not include people in their landscapes.

The figure interferes with the natural world, as I said earlier, and takes the focus off the beauty of the landscape. I like to bring them in because it brings a reality to the landscape: that people inhabit it. We build houses on it, we stand before it in awe, we feel we belong to it, and in some case we feel it belongs to us. I like how vulnerable the people look when they are alone in these portraits, standing before the vastness, and I believe this reflects how we often feel, or at least how I often feel, in the world at large. So small before it all.

You can hook a single solitary figure or a group of people in the foreground of your landscapes. Whatever you choose. I want to help guide you to create figures for your hooked rugs. We are often intimidated to try to draw people, because we see it as complicated. In many books on learning to draw, though, you will see that you can create a figure simply by drawing ovals and circles. This is how I taught myself to draw people. After discovering this, I bought myself a movable artist's figure model made of wood. I would pose this model and play with it.

But my best learning came from watching people. How they stand and how they moved. I liked to look at how they held their hands, the tilt of their head, the set of their shoulders. Just as I studied the landscape, I studied the movements of people. I remember being in yoga class and watching the woman across from me posing. I was so interested in the way she held herself and the way she moved that I could think only about my rugs. I was completely distracted.

When I hook rugs, I find it impossible to render an exact likeness of a person. The wool is too thick, or my hands are too clumsy to show a tiny face. When I go for detail when hooking people, it ends up looking like a caricature. I feel as if this cheapens the rug, particularly when it is a portrait in the landscape. I want the person to be a focal point but also to lead us into the space

◀ *What can you know about a person by the way they hold a fish?*, 29" × 27" (73.66 × 68.58 cm). The landscape in a rug informs the viewer and gives them a sense of place. It can also reinforce the subject matter, as you see here with three islands behind three women, who are each uniquely themselves.

▲ *Standing near the River*, 30" × 7" (76.2 × 17.78 cm). Water elements in your rug can be ponds, lakes, or rivers. What do you live near? Visit that body of water and try using it in your rugs. If you don't want to include water, the blue here could be gold or another shade of green, and it would work just as well.

behind them. So I try to hook people that fit into the space as well as stand out from it. Most often, the people I hook are not particular people. In some cases they feel a lot like self-portraiture.

The first thing to think about is perspective. Decide how big the person should be in the foreground. This of course depends on the size of the rug. You will notice that I often truncate people, showing just over half or three-quarters of the figure. This gives me some leeway with perspective and lets me show the figure larger than if I had to include the whole figure. You can then let the figure appear larger, and it gives me room to add more details to their pose and their clothing.

Then you can sketch the figure on the backing, most often to the left or the right of the scene behind them. Putting them a little off-center allows room for the landscape to be seen, and makes them slightly less important than if they were dead center. Be thoughtful about the placement of the figure in the landscape.

Once you have the figure sketched on the canvas, you can begin outlining them.

We talked earlier about how important outlining is for the landscape, and this is doubly true for people. The outline will create the shape of the person and the feeling they convey, so it is very important. Choose a single two-ply black yarn to outline people. Hook this outline by loosely skipping lots of holes. This allows you to convey shape but also lets the outline recede once the other colors are hooked around it. So, for example, when you hook the shoulders and arms and fill in her shirt color with red and put the grass in behind her, the black outline, because holes were skipped, will fade. If you hook it really tightly, the black lines will appear stiff and firm and somewhat higher. We will see the outline more than the shape of the figure. There is an exception to this loose outlining. If you are showing the bend of an arm or leg, you can hook the curve quite tightly for three or four stitches to emphasize it. Then you can start hooking loosely again.

I do not hook details in the faces, because I like the effect

▶ *The Yellow Bathing Suit*, 31" × 10" (78.74 × 25.4 cm). The details can make the difference between a beautiful rug and a dull one. You could add just a few flecks of pink or reds at the top of long grass and transform your rug. The flowers bounce off the yellow bathing suit and add a sense of balance to the piece.

that comes with using just shades of cream, tan, or brown. I choose a wool color that approximates the skin tone of the person I am hooking. Most often, the women in my rugs represent myself or my mother. I have chosen to use tan wool, but whatever color you choose, the method will be the same. I take two or three shades of tan, and I mix them randomly. I will then take the darkest or the lightest (it does not matter; I just want to create shading), and I will hook in small lines where the eyes, nose, and mouth would be. I will sometimes connect the line for the nose and mouth. I will then take the other one or two shades and hook around this. As I do, I try to hook the curve of the cheeks. When you are up close to it, it will not look like a face, but as you move away from the rug, there will be the intonation of facial features. I use the same color for any areas where skin tone is showing, such as on the arms, hands, or legs. One challenge you may face is separating the chin from the neck. Sometimes you can use a tiny bit of black yarn, or a deeper dark brown or dark tan, to outline the chin.

I try not to outline the face, so that the hair color is not separated from the face. For hair, sometimes use natural or carded fleece. This gives a natural look for hair. If you hook it high, the hair will appear full and curly, even a bit wild. If you want the hair to look more controlled, you can hook it low. There are many textured cloths and yarns that also work for hair. If you want the hair to appear straight, hook it low and linear.

If you are creating a small portrait of someone and you want it to look like them, it is important to capture some of their features. Simple things such as the way they hold their head, the set of their shoulders, how they hold their hands, hair color, and the way they dress will help us reflect them in wool.

Clothing is fun to hook. It is important to remember that the portrait must be in contrast to the landscape if you want it to stand out. It is difficult to hook a woman in a green dress standing in a green field. It just won't work well, even if the colors and textures are different. In rug hooking, we can add personality and make our portrait distinctive by the way we dress our people. Think of it as dressing dolls. You can dress the person in what you imagine they would like to wear.

Sometimes you can sketch a person roughly, drawing light ovals in pencil and then using a heavier pencil to draw their clothes on them. When you draw their clothes, think about the body underneath, the fullness of the hips, etc. This helps make the figure appear more natural. Again, in rug hooking you are not after realism with your figures. Instead, you want to create story and emotion when you add a figure to the landscape. A person on the landscape changes the whole story of the rug. Suddenly it becomes the story of "I was there" rather than the serenity of an empty field. It changes the rug completely, so think about it before you add a figure in your landscapes. Ask yourself what the story is that you want to tell in this rug. If adding a figure to the landscape can make it even more beautiful and more interesting, then I encourage you to try it.

▲ *Standing on Frozen Ground*, 17" × 17" (40.64 × 71.12 cm). This is a mood rug. Notice how the single figure is symbolically reflected in the island. The cream sky is a perfect example of not using blue for the sky. It adds to the solitude feel.

CONCLUSION

Hooking landscape rugs is painterly and process oriented. It takes an old tradition of using scraps of old clothing and burlap bags to create rugs for drafty floors and elevates it to art. Once, this craft was relegated as unimportant women's work. Something they did to keep their hands busy to pass the time. It was undervalued and seen as a chore of poverty. We have come to see it differently now. We have come to see it for what it is, a beautiful meditative art form that allows us to translate the world around us and create beauty every day. It is a craft that allows us to express ourselves, spend time with ourselves, build community, strengthen our imaginations, and deepen our ability to see the world. That tells me that this is a powerful craft, a powerful art form.

Throughout this book and in the rugs I have shown you here, you can see that landscape rug hooking offers you an opportunity not only to depict a place but to express how you feel about it and your relationship with it. Whether it is a few flowers in a patch of grass, your old homestead, or 70 acres alongside the highway, every place has a story, and every place has the possibility to capture our imagination. We live in these places and they are part of our story. Each of us has a powerful story to tell just for the simple fact that we are here in this time and place. Rug-hooking the landscape around you is a means to tell your story.

I am so excited for you. I love the idea that you will be looking at where you live and the places you love and dreaming of them in wool. I love that you will be using wool cloth and yarn to capture your imagination and bring the world around you home. I encourage you to just start. Just begin hooking your first simple landscape. Pull your first loops and do not worry about them being even or perfect. Just begin. Just hook. And as you do, let your hands and your body relax. Look at the colors on your frame and in the world around you and allow yourself to get lost in that, because this is a special place. It is a place where you can listen to yourself, a place where you can think and rest and grow. This place is your own personal landscape and it is waiting for you to immerse yourself in it.

A Special Bonus

Thank you for choosing this book. You're invited to 1 free workshop by Deanne Fitzpatrick on Landscape Rug Hooking. Use the QR code and this password: landscapelove2025

APPENDIX

Basic Beginner Instructions on Hooking a Rug

Hooking a rug is so easy. There is only one stitch to learn. Once you learn this stitch, it is really just about what you can do with color, texture, creativity, and design. These things, of course, are big things, and they make the possibilities for rug hooking limitless. But to get started, you really just need to learn how to hold your hook and pull those first loops.

Stretching Your Backing on a Frame

One of the things that makes rug hooking much easier is keeping your backing really taut. I like to stretch my linen so it is tight like a drum. Most rug hookers use a frame such as a sturdy quilting hoop to stretch their backing upon. They then hold it on their lap and hook their rug. You can also use an old wooden picture frame or an artist's stretcher bar and thumbtack your pattern to it. I like a floor-style frame called the Cheticamp frame, but you can also use a baby quilting frame.

You can find more detailed instructions, including a free course on how to hook rugs, on my website, hookingrugs.com.

Materials

Many people start rug hooking with a kit that has everything you need to get you started, but you do not have to. I like to use a mixture of yarn and cloth because it adds a lot of textures to the elements of the rug and makes the rug more interesting.

WOOL STRIPS

You can gather old wool clothing and sweaters and cut them into strips about ¼ inch wide and about 10 inches long. To make strips, take apart the clothing, wash and dry it, and then tear it into swatches that are about 4 inches by 10 inches. Then you can fold these pieces into four and, using 5½-inch scissors, cut the folded fabric into strips. The folding saves time and lets your strips pile up quickly.

YARN

You can also use yarn strands 10 to 15 inches long. I have an enormous stash of wool yarn that I have gathered over the years and that I dip into every day. I buy full skeins and cut both ends of the skein so that I can create a bundle of strips to hook. I then divide these strips into five or six sections and tie a single knot in each one. This keeps my yarn from becoming tangled messes. I then store these in open baskets by color and shades. It is expensive and takes time to build the big stash of colors that you need, so the best way is to add to it consistently over time. I also encourage you to ask your knitting friends if they have any leftover bits and pieces of wool yarn to add to your stash. They often have small bits and pieces of skeins left that will not work for a knitting project but might be perfect for a small section of your rug.

ESTIMATING HOW MUCH WOOL YOU NEED TO HOOK YOUR RUG

There is a simple way to estimate the amount of wool you need to hook a rug. You need four times the area of the size of the rug you want to hook. For example, if you wanted to hook a 4-by-4-inch square in red, you would need a piece of wool cloth to tear that is 4 by 16 inches This will usually leave you plenty of extra.

For wool yarn, it is more difficult. You can lay it over the area about four strands deep to get an estimate of how much of an area it will cover. Take a skein and flatten it out until it is about four strands in thickness, and see how big an area it will cover. You could also count how many strips of yarn you have once you cut your skein.

How to Hold Your Hook

Hold your hook comfortably in your hands. Do not grasp it too tightly; just hold it gently as if it was part of your hand itself. I like to hold my hook the way I held my pencil when I was a child learning to write longhand. The hook you choose should feel comfortable in your hand. I use the same hook for every width and weight of wool. I hold it on a 45-degree angle, but as I keep hooking it gets straighter and straighter, so that I am almost holding my hook straight up and down.

Preparing to hook: Hold your hook like a pencil in your dominant hand and thread your wool through your finger of your other hand.

How to Hook Your Rug

Hook like a pencil on the top side of your frame and put a strip of wool between your thumb and forefinger under the frame. Put the hook down through the hole in the burlap and catch the wool, pulling the end of the strip to the surface, using the hand underneath holding the wool, to help you guide it along. I don't use my hook to fish the wool from under the frame. Instead, I use the hand underneath the frame to feed the wool onto my hook. Both hands are working together, almost wrapping the wool around the hook underneath. Keep moving the hand underneath as you move your hand and hook along the top side. Do not hook too tightly.

How to hook: Put your hand holding the wool underneath your linen; push your hook down through the linen toward it; and bring up the wool to the surface.

Underneath: The hand underneath is helping the hand with the hook catch the wool so it can be brought to the surface loop by loop.

Skip a hole and put your hook down again and pull a loop up. Skip another hole and pull up another loop, letting your hand underneath move along as you pull your wool loop by loop. Keep hooking and be sure to skip some holes, because if you hook in every hole, the rug will be hooked too tightly and it will not lie flat. You do not have to skip every second or third hole; instead, create a random pattern of skipping holes.

Outlining and Filling In

Often in rug hooking, objects on your pattern are outlined, then filled in. This is the traditional way of hooking. So you can start by outlining the design if you like and then keep hooking it until it is filled in, or you can just go freestyle and begin hooking loops.

Blocking Your Rug

I am a big proponent of blocking rugs, because I believe that it in looking at our blocked work, we can really see what we did right and what we could do better, and learn. When you are finished hooking the total area of your rug, you can block it. This means that you take a piece of white cotton, such as an old sheet or a pillowcase, and soak it in a bowl of water. Wring it out with your hands to rid it of excess water, then lay it over your hooked rug. Then press it with a very hot iron. You can do it on the top side or both sides. Blocking evens out your loops and gives the rug a nice finish.

Binding Your Rug

I always make sure I leave 3 inches or so of excess linen around my pattern, so that when I have finished hooking, it I can fold these pieces over, hiding the raw edges in the fold, and hand-sew this extra fabric to the back with a linen-colored thread. It is like hemming your rug. In the corners, I fold and tightly sew one piece of linen over the other so that the corners are neat. If I am planning to frame my rug in a wooden frame, as I often do, I just serge the edge of the linen about 1½ inches from where my hooking ends, and then I hand-sew it to the back of the rug without folding over the fabric, so that it will lie flatter in the frame.

Framing Your Rug

If you decide to frame your rug make sure that you have a frame that is approximately ⅛ to ¼ inch bigger than your rug. Wool blooms a bit and spreads so leave a little extra room. I use frames that are built like a box and have a wooden back. To attach the rug, I use a staple gun to attach the rug to the frame. I try to open the hooking and squeeze the staple in between the loops so that they are hidden and you cannot see them. I avoid using glue because when you glue the rug to the frame you cannot take it out easily and you can no longer repair the rug or change a color should you want to. Stapling works much better than glue.

▶ Deanne outside her studio, which she has run for 35 years in downtown Amherst, Nova Scotia.

to belong
that I am here
I make art so you will
know that I was here
I make art
the ballad
of freshwater

INDEX

DEANNE FITZPATRICK is an artist, entrepreneur, and transformative rug hooker who for more than thirty years has owned and operated the Deanne Fitzpatrick Studio. Her designs, supplies, and kits are available worldwide. Deanne teaches her craft both in-person and virtually, and she has fostered and nourished a vibrant community of rug hookers from all over the world.

She has been awarded the prestigious Order of Canada for her work in the advancement of rug hooking as an art form and was named Rug Hooker of the Year by the Rug Hooking Museum of North America. She was awarded an honorary doctorate from Mount Saint Vincent University. Deanne's work has been featured in solo exhibits at the Art Gallery of Nova Scotia and is found in private and public collections, including those of the Canadian Museum of History and the Nova Scotia Art Bank.

Her many previous books on creativity and rug hooking include *Simply Modern: Contemporary Designs for Hooked Rugs; Inspired Rug-Hooking: Turning Atlantic Canadian Life into Art;* and *Sunday Letters.*

hookingrugs.com